Dedication

I SEEM TO HAVE BEEN BORN WITH A HEART FOR THE PEOPLE OF ISRAEL. Perhaps it came from my love of the Bible, which I discovered at age nine.

I was particularly fascinated with King David, who danced before the Lord in joyful adoration.[1] David was the first king to unite all the tribes of Israel. They came to him and said, "We are thy bone and thy flesh,"[2] a statement one could only make in a familial context, for surely, after all, the tribes of Israel are all related by blood as the children of Abraham and Sarah, Isaac and Rebekah, and Jacob and his wives, Rachel and Leah.

Before David, the tribes fought one another as only bickering brothers can. David loved his people, but he loved God even more. David was determined to unite Israel and form them as a holy nation under God, with a temple at its center. The Lord called David "a man after his own heart"[3] and promised David that the Messiah would come through his loins. This promise was, and has been, the great hope of Israel: that while David was unable to keep the tribes united, Messiah will.

This book is dedicated to David and to the Messiah ben David, Yeshua, Jesus Christ. May we prepare our hearts for the longed-for unification of the tribes of Israel, with our Messiah as King.

1. 2 Samuel 6:14.
2. 2 Samuel 5:1.
3. 1 Samuel 13:14.

Other books by Lynda Cherry

The Redemption of the Bride:
God's Redeeming Love for His Covenant People

The Feasts and Festivals of the Messiah

A Passover Seder Script for Christian Families

Judah AND *Joseph* REUNITED

THE HOPE FOR ISRAEL

Judah and Joseph Reunited

The Hope for Israel

LYNDA CHERRY

CFI
AN IMPRINT OF CEDAR FORT, INC.
SPRINGVILLE, UTAH

ISBN 13: 978-1-4621-4564-5

Published by CFI, an imprint of Cedar Fort, Inc.
2373 W. 700 S., Suite 100, Springville, UT 84663
Distributed by Cedar Fort, Inc., www.cedarfort.com

Library of Congress Control Number: 2023930789

Cover design by Courtney Proby

Printed in the United States of America

10 9 8 7 6 5 4 3 2 1

Printed on acid-free paper

Contents

Introduction

Born out of order, neither Judah nor Joseph expected to receive the firstborn birthright from Father Jacob (Israel), yet each was endowed with powerful blessings of leadership over his siblings. Judah was given the right of kingship and promised that the Messiah would come through his loins.[1] Joseph was given the blessings of the birthright and the charge to save all of Israel, starting with his own eleven brothers.[2]

Because he had the birthright blessings, which includes priesthood leadership and a double portion of his father's inheritance, Joseph's two sons, Ephraim and Manasseh, inherited those blessings from their father, Joseph, with Ephraim receiving the greater share and the birthright.[3] Thus, often as we read the scriptures, we see Ephraim's name used instead of Joseph's, which can cause some confusion. One such example was Isaiah's prophecy that in the last days "Ephraim shall not envy Judah, and Judah shall not vex Ephraim."[4] In this case, the name "Ephraim" represents the tribe of Joseph, and as we shall see, the ancient prophets counted Joseph, Ephraim, and Manasseh as one.

Both Judah and Joseph (or Ephraim) had patriarchal blessings that promised leadership over the other tribes of Israel, and this fact led to

1. Genesis 49:8–12.
2. Genesis 49:22–26; 50:17–20.
3. Genesis 48:17–19; Deuteronomy 33:16–17.
4. Isaiah 11:13.

a constant state of friction between the two brothers and their descendants. Who was supposed to be in charge—Judah or Joseph? This friction led to the eventual division of Israel. Rehoboam, Solomon's son and a descendant of Judah, remained on the throne in Jerusalem, while Jeroboam, of Ephraim, encouraged ten of the tribes to follow him. Jeroboam's kingdom became known as the Northern Kingdom of Israel, with its capital in Samaria.

Jeroboam feared that he would lose his people if they went to worship at the temple in Jerusalem. Therefore, he set up two golden calves that he called *Jehovah* at the northern and southern boundaries of his kingdom. Any believers in the *real* Jehovah and His temple separated themselves and moved southward into the kingdom now known as Judah, with Jerusalem as its capital. Thus, the northern ten tribes were led into apostasy because of the division between Judah and Ephraim, which resulted in their destruction, captivity, and scattering throughout the world.[5]

In that scattering, Joseph's patriarchal blessing that promised he would be as "a fruitful bough . . . whose branches run over the wall"[6] began to be fulfilled. Through multiple dispersions, Joseph's posterity were taken throughout the earth, which included the family of Lehi, who left Jerusalem and were led to the New World at the time of the Babylonian captivity of the Jews.[7]

The Jews, or Judah, in the meanwhile held strong for many generations until King Manasseh led the country into idolatry, and their destruction was assured.[8] The subsequent Babylonian captivity of the Jews brought out a strength of will that united the Jews as never before and produced a fierce determination to remain uniquely bound as a covenant people who rigorously kept the commandments of God.

The long isolation and separation of the tribes has resulted in a complete disassociation between the tribes of Israel, a breach that must be repaired. The gathering of Israel—all of its tribal members—is

---

5. See 1 Kings 12.
6. Genesis 49:22.
7. 1 Nephi 1–2.
8. 2 Kings 21:11–16.

essential, and Judah and Joseph as the leading tribes must join together and lead in that process.

Judah has preserved the sacred records of the covenant, and the Judaic Messiah has provided the means and the power through which the gathering can occur. And before Moses died, he prophesied that Joseph would have a specific role in the gathering of the latter days. He said:

> Let the blessing come upon the head of Joseph, and upon the top of the head of him that was separated from his brethren. His glory is like the firstling of his bullock, and his horns are like the horns of unicorns:[9] with them he shall push the people together to the ends of the earth.[10]

The hope *of* Israel is in the Jewish Messiah, Yeshua, or Jesus Christ. The hope *for* Israel is that the individual tribes come to themselves, remember their heritage, and unite once again as a covenant family. In that work, Judah and Joseph must heal the breach and lead the way.

9. Hebrew: the wild ox, the sign for the tribe of Ephraim.
10. Deuteronomy 33:16–17.

CHAPTER 1

Who Is Israel?

ISRAEL IS THE NAME OF GOD'S COVENANT FAMILY.

The New and Everlasting Covenant

The first covenants were made with Adam and Eve and successive generations, including Enoch, Noah, Melchizedek, Abraham, and Isaac. The covenants they embraced were the same covenants included in *The New and Everlasting Covenant.* The New and Everlasting Covenant is "the fulness of the gospel of Jesus Christ."[1]

> It is new every time it is revealed following a period of apostasy. It is everlasting in the sense that it is God's covenant and has been enjoyed in every gospel dispensation where people have been willing to receive it.[2]

> The fulness of the gospel is called The New and Everlasting Covenant. It includes the covenants made at baptism, during the sacrament, in the temple, and at any other time. The Lord calls it everlasting because it is ordained by an everlasting God and because the covenant will never be changed. He gave this same covenant to Adam, Enoch, Noah, Abraham, and other prophets. In this sense it

1. Doctrine and Covenants 66:2.
2. Guide to the Scriptures, "New and Everlasting Covenant," churchofjesuschrist.org.

is not new. But the Lord calls it new because each time the gospel is restored after being taken from the earth, it is new to the people who receive it.[3]

Father Abraham

Abraham is often remembered as "the father of the faithful" and "as the head of the covenant line, which is personified in the house of Israel."[4]

Abraham and his wife, Sarah, demonstrated obedience and faith as they left their home in Haran to keep the commandments of the Lord. Their faith was tested to its limits when the Lord asked Abraham to sacrifice their son, Isaac. According to the author of Hebrews, Abraham believed that God would raise Isaac from the dead in order to fulfill the promises He had given Abraham that the families of the earth would be blessed through his posterity.[5] Isaac also showed great faith in that offering, for it is believed that Isaac was a young adult and could have overpowered his aged father if he were unwilling to be the sacrifice the Lord had asked for.

The faith passed from parent to child is crucial to our understanding of the formation of Israel as the covenant family. The Lord praised Abraham, saying:

> For I know him, that he will command his children and his household after him, and they shall keep the way of the Lord, to do justice and judgment; that the Lord may bring upon Abraham that which he hath spoken of him.[6]

How was the Lord to accomplish his promise that through Abraham's posterity "all the families of the earth [would be] blessed"[7] if Abraham's posterity lost hold of the covenant in the first generations? In order for Isaac to be the fulfillment of the birthright son,

---

3. "The Lord's Covenant People," *Gospel Principles*, 85.
4. "Abraham: Father of the Faithful," *Ensign*, February 2006.
5. Hebrews 11:17–19.
6. Genesis 18:19.
7. Abraham 2:11.

Isaac would need to cherish his own relationship with the Lord and the covenants the Lord was offering.

Isaac and the Covenant Promises

Indeed, Isaac *did* fulfill his earlier promise of faithfulness and developed his own personal relationship with God. Therefore, the Lord appeared to him and renewed the covenant promise to Isaac that He had made with his father, Abraham.[8] These covenant promises are important to understand so that we also know what promises we may obtain as children of the covenant. They include

- A knowledge of the fulness of the gospel and the Plan of Salvation
- A land of promise, an inheritance given by the Lord
- A fruitful posterity—eternal families
- The priesthood of God, through which the blessings can be realized[9]

Jacob and the Covenant Birthright

Isaac had twin sons, one of whom—Jacob—earned the birthright privileges through his own obedience and faithfulness. Jacob is described as a "plain" man, which the footnote describes in the Hebrew as "whole, complete, perfect, simple, plain."[10] The older son, Esau, is described as a "cunning hunter"[11] who disregarded the covenant obligations of the Lord by marrying outside of the covenant and joining himself to women who worshipped other gods.[12] The scriptures tell us that "Esau despised his birthright,"[13] yet he was full of anger and bitterness when his brother Jacob was given that blessing.

---

8. See Genesis 26:2–4, 23.
9. See Abraham 2:8–11.
10. See footnote for Genesis 25:27.
11. Genesis 25:27.
12. Genesis 26:34–35.
13. Genesis 25:34.

While some believe that Jacob obtained the birthright through trickery—first selling a meal to his brother for it[14] and later disguising himself as Esau to obtain it from his father, Isaac[15]—it's important to recognize that the Lord had told Rebekah, their mother, that the younger son would be the birthright child even while they were still in the womb.[16] Lest the significance of that prophecy be diminished, we must consider the fact that the day after the deception in Isaac's tent, Isaac once again blessed Jacob with all of the blessings of the birthright, including the priesthood and the Abrahamic covenant, this time knowing full well which son he was bestowing the blessing upon.

Ironically, neither Isaac nor Esau ended up sacrificing any of their wealth or lands for Jacob. Jacob served in Haran for twenty years under Rebekah's brother Laban and there acquired great wealth through his diligence insomuch that he gifted Esau an abundance of cattle[17] and purchased his own lands as he made his journey back to Hebron. Esau also had thrived during that twenty-year absence and lacked for nothing.[18]

Jacob's Name Changed to Israel

The Lord had preordained Jacob for his all-important role as the father of Israel. As Jacob left his father's land to find a wife who honored the covenant, the Lord appeared to him, and as He had done with Abraham and Isaac, personally endowed Jacob with all of the covenant blessings.[19] Many years, two wives, two concubines, and eleven sons later, Jacob encountered an angel on his way back home to his inheritance and his brother, Esau. After "wrestling" with the angel all night, the angel left a blessing upon Jacob and changed his name to Israel. The angel explained, "Thy name shall be called no more Jacob,

14. Genesis 25:30–33.
15. Genesis 27:5–30.
16. Genesis 25:23.
17. Genesis 33:8–10.
18. Genesis 33:17–19.
19. Genesis 28:10–15.

but Israel: for as a prince hast thou power with God and with men, and hast prevailed."[20]

Through Jacob, the great family of *Israel* had begun. We will note that like their progenitors before them, they are a human family comprised of everyday mortals who experienced petty jealousy, feelings of revenge, despair, and favoritism. As symbolized by Jacob's wrestle with the angel, these mortals wrestled with themselves, and sometimes with God, in order to see clearly and fulfill their destiny. In his youth, Joseph seemed to be a braggart, and Judah sold his brother into captivity. Yet each, as we shall see, matured and overcame the foibles of youth, as well as the challenges and trials of manhood.

20. Genesis 32:28.

CHAPTER 2

Twelve Sons, Twelve Tribes

Jacob Marries within the Covenant

WHEN JACOB ARRIVED AT HIS MOTHER'S BIRTHPLACE IN HARAN, THE first woman he saw was his cousin Rachel. Like Rebekah before her, she was industriously engaged in watering animals near the village well.[1] Jacob had made a long journey to find a wife who would be his partner in keeping the covenants of the Lord and raising a family to honor those covenants. That journey had been fruitful in that Jacob fell in love with Rachel immediately and found favor with her brother, Laban.[2] But Rachel had an older sister, who, according to tradition, must be married first. "Leah was tender eyed; but Rachel was beautiful and well favored."[3] The *but* in that description is heartbreaking and foreshadows the sorrow that Leah must have borne throughout her life as she was constantly compared to her sister.

I've often wondered if, like Jacob and Esau, Rachel and Leah were twins. I've wondered if God prepared two sisters for two brothers, one of whom disdained the covenant and married Hittite women who

1. Genesis 24:15–20; 29:1–10.
2. Genesis 29:13–14.
3. Genesis 29:17.

did not know Jehovah.[4] The journey to find a wife of the covenant was a long one. Abraham's servant had made it for the sake of Isaac,[5] and Jacob now had done the same. Was it simply too much for Esau, which then left Leah unmatched and doomed to always feel second best to Rachel? If Leah and Rachel *were* twins, it might explain why Jacob did not recognize her on their wedding day when her father, Laban, forced Leah to wed Jacob in Rachel's stead, heavily veiled as was custom, but enough like Rachel to deceive Jacob.[6]

Jacob worked in Laban's fields for seven years in order to win Rachel. "They seemed unto him but a few days, for the love he had to her."[7]

He had no such love for Leah, and all knew it. Laban demanded that Jacob serve him another seven years after his wedding to Leah, and Jacob fulfilled that demand, for "he loved Rachel more than Leah."[8]

Leah and Rachel: Mothers of the Family of Israel

What followed the union of Jacob to the two sisters was a painful competition to provide him with children. One of the covenant promises is to have a fruitful posterity—and both sisters were determined to fulfill that promise.

According to scripture, "the Lord saw that Leah was hated, [and] opened her womb"[9] first. She bore a son named Reuben.

> For she said, Surely the Lord hath looked upon my affliction; now therefore my husband will love me.[10]
>
> And she conceived again, and bare a son; and said, Because the Lord hath heard that I was hated, he hath therefore given me this son also: and she called his name Simeon. And she conceived again, and bare a son; and said, Now this time will my husband be joined unto

---

4. Genesis 26:34–35.
5. See Genesis 24.
6. Genesis 29:23–25.
7. Genesis 29:20.
8. Genesis 29:30.
9. Genesis 29:31.
10. Genesis 29:32.

> me, because I have born him three sons: therefore was his name called Levi. And she conceived again, and bare a son: and she said, Now will I praise the Lord: therefore she called his name Judah; and left bearing.[11]

Rachel was distressed and full of envy over her sister's fruitfulness. In her desperation, she asked Jacob to marry her handmaid, Bilhah, and have children by her that Rachel would claim as her own. Bilhah *did* conceive, and another son was born, whom Rachel named Dan. Yet again, Rachel sent Bilhah to Jacob, and Bilhah conceived and gave birth to Naphtali.[12]

The conception war between the sisters escalated. Following Rachel's example, Leah gave *her* handmaid, Zilpah, to Jacob as a wife, and Zilpah gave birth to Gad and then Asher.[13] Rachel then made a bargain with Leah that if Leah's son, Reuben, would give Rachel mandrakes known for aiding fertility, then Rachel would send Jacob in to Leah.

It's hard to imagine Jacob's feelings as the wives sent him back and forth in their jealousy. Nevertheless, Leah *did* give birth to another son in the bargain she had made with Rachel: Issachar.[14] In a desperate hope that because she had given him the most sons Jacob would live with *her*, Leah finally gave birth to a sixth son, Zebulun, and then to a daughter, Dinah.[15]

After all of these births—ten sons, and one daughter—Rachel finally conceived and gave birth to Joseph.[16] Some time later, after Jacob and Esau were reconciled and Jacob had taken his family away from Haran and back to Hebron, Rachel gave birth to her second son, Benjamin, and died in the process.[17]

The following chart lists the children born to Jacob by each mother:

---

11. Genesis 29:33–35.
12. Genesis 30:1–8.
13. Genesis 30:9–13.
14. Genesis 30:14–18.
15. Genesis 30:19–21.
16. Genesis 30:22–24.
17. Genesis 35:16–19.

Leah	Zilpah	Rachel	Bilhah
Reuben	Gad	Joseph	Dan
Simeon	Asher	Benjamin	Naphtali
Levi			
Judah			
Issachar			
Zebulun			
Dinah			

Deceit and Murder within Jacob's Family

Jacob, with his burgeoning family and flocks, at last dwelt in the land promised to Abraham, but there were other Canaanite inhabitants there as well. While Abraham's posterity were meant to be a blessing to the families of the earth, one event illustrates how Simeon and Levi perverted that instruction to instead produce death, destruction, and enmity.

Shechem, the son of a prince of the Hivites, fell in love with Dinah, Jacob's daughter by Leah. He lay with her and "defiled her"[18] but earnestly desired to marry her. His father spoke in Shechem's behalf, asking Jacob for Dinah's hand in marriage. More, he asked that there might be a full family alliance, with marriages of sons and daughters between both families, with his own family providing rich lands and treasure as a bride-price.

Jacob's sons answered Shechem and his father "deceitfully,"[19] for they had devised a most terrible plan: they convinced Shechem, his father, and all of the men of the city to be circumcised because an Israelite was required to comply with this as a token of the Abrahamic Covenant. The account explains that Shechem was an honorable man, and he was glad to acquiesce to the requirement. But on the third day, when all of the men of the city were incapacitated with pain, according

18. Genesis 34:1–2.
19. Genesis 34:13.

to their previously laid plan, Simeon and Levi (Dinah's brothers) came with swords in hand and killed every man in the city. In addition, they plundered and carried away all of the women, children, cattle, and wealth of those they had murdered.[20]

Jacob was horrified by his sons' deceit and murder of the Hivites and feared that all of the Canaanites in the land would turn against him and his family.[21] His horror over their actions is reflected in the patriarchal blessings he gave to Simeon and Levi years later, just before his death. He called them "instruments of cruelty" and said, "Cursed be their anger, for it was fierce; and their wrath, for it was cruel: I will divide them in Jacob, and scatter them in Israel."[22]

Reuben, the Oldest, Brings Dishonor to His Father and Family

Jacob's firstborn son, Reuben, brought another cause for heartbreak to Jacob and Leah by sleeping with his father's concubine, Bilhah.[23] Bilhah had been Rachel's handmaid and had married Jacob at Rachel's urging. Bilhah had given birth to two sons, Reuben's half-brothers, Dan and Naphtali. What would tempt Reuben to defile her, for surely this must have been a case of force on Reuben's part?

There may have been two goals driving Reuben's actions: According to ancient custom, when a king or ruler died, his eldest son was given possession of all that he had—including his wives and concubines. When Absalom was trying to usurp his father King David's throne, he set up a tent on top of the palace and slept with his father's concubines "in the sight of all of Israel" so they could see his disdain for his father and as a sign that he was claiming his right to the throne.[24] Reuben may have been asserting his right as the firstborn and birthright son by preempting his father's formal acknowledgment of that claim, but, like Absalom, he was also exhibiting a total disrespect for his father

20. Genesis 34:13–29.
21. Genesis 34:30.
22. Genesis 49:5–7.
23. Genesis 35:22.
24. 2 Samuel 16:22.

and his family and the covenant of holiness that should have set him apart from the traditions of other cultures.

The second issue that may lie behind Reuben's desecration of Bilhah was Reuben's (and Leah's?) desire that Bilhah not take Rachel's place as the favorite wife. A few verses earlier in the account relate the fact that Rachel died giving birth to Benjamin.[25] All of the family knew that Rachel was the favorite. Were Leah and her sons worried that Bilhah, Rachel's companion and handmaid, would now take on the favored status? If Reuben had defiled her, there was no possibility of that occurring. The intimate relationship between Jacob and Bilhah would be destroyed.

The Talmud seems to provide yet another possible explanation for Reuben's interaction with Bilhah that does not include any sexual immorality on Reuben's part. It explains that

> Reuben moved Jacob's bed from Bilhah's tent to the tent of his mother, Leah. Reuben knew that Jacob loved Rachel more than his mother and that it was she who Jacob desired to marry at the outset. Jacob kept his marriage bed in Rachel's tent for the duration of her life. After Rachel's passing, Reuben assumed that Jacob would move into Leah's tent. In his mind, Bilhah and Zilpah were inferior to Rachel and Leah, their former masters. When Jacob chose to move into Bilhah's tent instead, he felt righteous indignation. "If my mother's sister was my mother's rival, should my mother's sister's handmaid be her rival as well?" He took Jacob's bed and moved it to Leah's tent.[26]

Reuben lost his birthright status as a result of his sin. This is reflected in Jacob's patriarchal blessing to Reuben where Jacob states:

> Reuben, thou art my firstborn, my might, and the beginning of my strength, the excellency of dignity, and the excellency of power: Unstable as water, thou shalt not excel; because thou wentest up to thy father's bed, then defiledst thou it: he went up to my couch.[27]

---

25. Genesis 35:18–19.
26. Shabbat 55b; see www.sefaria.org/Shabbat.55b?lang=bi.
27. Genesis 49:3–4.

Jacob's admonition against Reuben does seem to imply something more serious than simply moving his father's bed from one tent to another.

According to Daniel Ludlow:

> Custom and tradition indicated that the first wife should have precedence over the other wives; thus it was determined that the firstborn son of the first wife should be the birthright son as long as he proved worthy. Only in case of unworthiness or death would the birthright go to the firstborn son of the second wife. No second-born sons were considered for the birthright unless all firstborn sons proved to be unworthy.[28]

In the next chapter we will explore the meaning of the birthright and also the fact that the birthright in this family ended up going to Rachel's firstborn son, Joseph. For now, as we account for—and count—the sons of Israel, or Jacob, we note that the author of Chronicles confirms the fact that because of Reuben's sin, his birthright privileges were given to his brother Joseph and through Joseph to his sons Ephraim and Manasseh.[29]

Counting in Ephraim and Manasseh—How Do Thirteen Add Up to Twelve?

As the inclusion of Joseph's sons Ephraim and Manasseh often throws people off in the counting of the twelve tribes, it is important to understand that they are included *as one* in Joseph's stead. This may be particularly confusing when we recognize that Ephraim is given the birthright leadership role within that duality while still being counted as one with Manasseh. Moses illustrated this clearly when he pronounced blessings upon the individual tribes, and when it came to Joseph's turn, he included Joseph, Ephraim, and Manasseh as one.[30]

---

28. "What laws governed the inheritance of birthright in the Old Testament?," *Ensign*, September 1980.
29. 1 Chronicles 5:1–2.
30. Deuteronomy 33:13–17.

Joshua, when making land assignments, also referred to the three as one people.[31]

The following chart shows each son of Israel, the meaning behind his name, his patriarchal blessing, and the symbol of his tribe. It also includes Moses's blessing on each tribe, its land allotment in Israel, and the important events in its history. Note that despite the sins committed by individuals within the tribe (including the original twelve sons that the tribes are named after), each tribe is noted as having a place in the celestial kingdom except Dan's. We should not read too much into this fact, however, because when the book of Revelation describes the twelve gates of the celestial city, each gate is named for one of the twelve tribes of Israel, including Dan's.[32]

The celestial city and its gates and foundations each bore a name for each of the tribes of Israel, and likewise, the ancient breastplate of the high priest also bore a precious stone for each of the tribes with their name engraved upon it. In addition, the high priest carried the names upon his shoulders, where they were engraved once again upon precious stones, six on each shoulder.[33] There is some disagreement as to what those precious stones were and to which tribe they were assigned.[34] As a result, the stones are not included in the chart below. What is important to recognize is the Lord's explanation for the purpose of the stones and the names: "And Aaron [the high priest] shall bear the names of the children of Israel in the breastplate of judgment upon his heart, when he goeth in unto the holy place, for a memorial before the Lord continually."[35]

Each name is precious before the Lord, our great High Priest, who bears the names upon His heart continually. None of the tribes are considered a "throw-away" tribe. Each son of Israel and each tribe is of infinite worth to God. The command to gather Israel does not leave any left out or unaccounted for. Like the lost lamb, each is precious to the Shepherd of Israel. Each has a role to play, as suggested in their

---

31. Joshua 17:17.
32. Revelation 21:12.
33. Exodus 28:12, 15–21.
34. See Yehuda Altein's "The High Priest's Breastplate (Choshen)."
35. Exodus 28:29.

individual patriarchal blessings. In those blessings, both Judah and Joseph were given roles of leadership for the family of Israel, which will be discussed further and in detail. As we shall see, their mission is to assist God in "saving" and uniting Israel.

TWELVE SONS OF JACOB: NAMES, PATRIARCHAL BLESSINGS, and LAND INHERITANCES

Name/Meaning	Patriarchal Blessing	Land Allotment	Events
Reuben, "See, a Son" **Symbol: Man or Mandrake**	The beginning of Jacob's strength and excellency, but unstable and will not excel. Gen. 49:3–4	East of the Jordan River with Gad, and "East" Manasseh. Josh. 13:15–23	Lost birthright to sons of Joseph for defiling his father's bed. 1 Chron. 5:1; JST Gen. 48:5
	Let him live with many for posterity. Deut. 33:6		Convinced his brothers *not* to kill Joseph and later offered his sons as guarantee that he would bring Benjamin back safely to Joseph in Egypt. Gen. 37:21; 42:37
Simeon, "Hearing" **Symbol: Tower or City of Shechem**	An instrument of cruelty, will be divided and scattered in Israel. Gen. 49:5–7	Tribe of Simeon given a portion of the land of Judah. Josh. 19:1–9	Simeon and Levi slay a neighboring tribe. Gen. 34:25–31
		Tribe of Simeon given a portion of the land of Israel in Ezekiel's vision of the future. Ezek. 48:24	Tribe of Simeon joined with Judah and Joseph in conquering the Canaanites. Judg. 1

Name/Meaning	Patriarchal Blessing	Land Allotment	Events
			His descendants are known as mighty men of war. 1 Chron. 12:25
			Simeon's posterity in the celestial kingdom. Rev. 7:7
Levi, "Joined" **Symbol: Breastplate, Urim and Thummim**	An instrument of cruelty, will be divided and scattered in Israel. Gen. 49:5–7	No inheritance in the land save service in the temple; they receive a tithing from the people. Numb. 18:21, 23–24	Simeon and Levi slay a neighboring tribe. Gen. 34:25–31
	Let the Urim and Thummim be in their care; they have observed the word of the Lord and kept His covenant. Deut. 33:8–11		Levites to administer in the tabernacle and temple. Numb. 3:5–10; Levites "offered as an offering of the children of Israel," set apart by Aaron, given to the Lord in place of all firstborn sons. Numb. 8:7–16
			Levi blessed with priesthood, urim and thummim, and so forth. Deut. 33:8–11

Name/Meaning	Patriarchal Blessing	Land Allotment	Events
			Sons of Levi to offer an offering in righteousness in the latter days/ Millennium. D&C 13:1
			Levi's posterity in the celestial kingdom. Rev. 7:7
			Moses from Levi
Judah, "Praise" **Symbol: Lion**	His brethren will praise and bow down to him; like a lion; the scepter of Israel shall be his until the Messiah; prophecies of the Savior, who will come through his lineage. Gen. 49:8–12	Judah is given their portion in the southern kingdom, Jerusalem the capital. Josh. 15	King David from Judah; king first of Judah, then of all of Israel; the royal tribe. 2 Sam. 2:11
	The Lord will keep him strong and help him against enemies. Deut. 33:7		Only Judah left as a whole tribe after the destruction of Israel. 2 Kings 17:18
	Enmity between Ephraim, Manasseh, and Judah. Isa. 9:21		Judah's posterity in the celestial kingdom. Rev. 7:5

Name/Meaning	Patriarchal Blessing	Land Allotment	Events
Dan, "To Judge" **Symbol: Eagle with a Serpent in its Talons or Pair of Scales**	A judge of the people; a serpent and adder to those along the path. Gen. 49:16–18	Last tribe to receive a land allotment. They did not like the land given to them, so they attacked another city and took it over. Their new land was in northern boundary of Israel. Judg. 18	Held at bay by the Amorites; not able to drive them out of the land. Judg. 1:34
	A lion's whelp that shall leap from Bashan. Deut. 33:22		Set up false idols from the time they took their lands in Israel. Judg. 18:30–31
			Location of false idol set up by Jeroboam. 1 Kings 12:29
			The golden calves of Jeroboam remained in Dan. 2 Kings 10:29
Naphtali, "Wrestling" **Symbol: Hind; Deer**	A hind let loose; gives goodly words. Gen. 49:21	Land surrounding the Sea of Galilee. Josh. 19:32–39	Naphtali's posterity in the celestial kingdom. Rev. 7:6
	Satisfied with favor and full of the blessings of the Lord. Deut. 33:23		

Name/Meaning	Patriarchal Blessing	Land Allotment	Events
Gad, "A Troop" **Symbol: Troop of Horsemen**	A troop shall overcome him, but he shall overcome at last. Gen. 49:19	Did not want to cross Jordan; wanted to stay in the land of the Canaanites because of their cattle; allied with tribe of Reuben and "East" Manasseh. Numb. 32:1–5; Deut. 3:12–20	Mighty warriors; went after false gods; destroyed by Assyria. 1 Chron. 5:18–26
	He dwells as a lion tearing the arm with the crown of the head. He was a lawgiver, and gave the first portion to himself. Deut. 33:20–21		Gad's posterity in the celestial kingdom. Rev. 7:5
Asher, "My Happiness" **Symbol: Cup or Olive Tree**	His bread shall be fat and he shall eat royal dainties. Gen. 49:20	Shared inherited land with Manasseh; settled in the northwest, bordering on the Mediterranean and the Phoenician Empire; associated with seafaring. Joshua 17:7, 10–11; 19:24–31; Judg. 5	Heeded the call of King Hezekiah to come to Passover and renew covenants. 2 Chron. 30:11
	Blessed with children; dip feet in oil; shoes like iron and brass. Deut. 33:24–29 (Asher's land was rich with olive orchards. Wealthy.)		Asher's posterity in the celestial kingdom. Rev. 7:6

Name/Meaning	Patriarchal Blessing	Land Allotment	Events
Issachar, "A Reward" **Symbol: Ass or Sun, Moon, and Stars**	Compared to an ass between two burdens; saw that rest was good and the land pleasant and gave his shoulder to tribute; became a servant. Gen. 49:14–15	Primarily in the Jezreel Valley, between the tribes of Zebulun and Naphtali, the slopes of the eastern portion of lower Galilee. Josh. 19:17–23	Known for their wisdom; instrumental in the tribes uniting under King David; accepted the call of Hezekiah to come to Passover and renew covenants. 1 Chron. 12:32; 2 Chron. 30:18
	Issachar safe in his tents; shall offer sacrifices of righteousness, reap the treasures of the seas. Deut. 33:18–19		Issachar's posterity in the celestial kingdom. Rev. 7:7
Zebulun, "Dwelling" **Symbol: Ship**	Shall dwell at the haven of the sea with many ships. Gen. 49:13	Confused accounts about location. Patriarchal blessing says inheritance by the sea. Joshua 19:10–16 states Zebulun bordered on all sides by other tribes. No account of the sea or Galilee.	Lived amongst the Canaanites and became subject to forced labor. Judges 1:30
	Have abundance of the sea and treasures hid in the sand; offer righteous sacrifices. Deut. 33:18–19 (same as Issachar)		Heeded the call of King Hezekiah to come to Passover and renew covenants. 2 Chron. 30:11

Name/Meaning	Patriarchal Blessing	Land Allotment	Events
			Zebulun's posterity in the celestial kingdom. Rev. 7:8
Joseph, "Adding" **Symbol: Sheaf of Wheat**	Fruitful bough, branches run over the wall; made strong by the Lord although he was vexed and persecuted; blessed above (heaven) and below (earth); blessings of breast and womb; his blessings will prevail to the utmost hills.	Joseph's double-portion birthright was passed on to Ephraim (birthright) and Manasseh. See their inheritance below.	Joseph sold into Egypt by his brothers; he rose to power as a trusted advisor to Pharaoh and saved Israel during a famine.
	Blessed of the Lord be his land, for the precious things of heaven, for the dew, and for the deep . . . for precious fruits brought forth by the sun and the precious things put forth by the moon; for the chief things of the ancient mountains, and for the precious things of the everlasting hills, and for the precious things of the earth and fulness thereof. Deut. 33:13–16		

Name/Meaning	Patriarchal Blessing	Land Allotment	Events
	Joseph prevailed and obtained the birthright through obedience and righteousness; he shall be a light to Israel and deliver Israel from captivity and bondage and bring salvation unto them. JST Gen. 48:5–11		
	A promise that a fruitful branch shall come from Joseph; a prophet from Joseph's loins (not the Messiah) shall rise up to deliver the people from bondage; a branch shall be carried to a far country and will be remembered in the covenants of the Lord; in the latter days they shall bring forth light and help deliver Israel from captivity; a seer from Joseph's loins shall be raised up who shall be called Joseph; he will bring people back to a knowledge of the covenants and do a great work; he will bring the word of Joseph's seed to all the world and join with the word of Judah to confound false doctrine. JST Gen. 50:24–26; 2 Nephi 3:4–22		

Name/Meaning	Patriarchal Blessing	Land Allotment	Events
Benjamin "Son of My Right Hand" **Symbol: Wolf**	Like a ravening wolf in the morning, will divide the spoil in the evening. Gen. 49:27	Land given between Ephraim to the north and Judah to the south, prime location; Bethel, Jerusalem, Jericho—three holy cities given to Benjamin to share with Judah. Josh. 18:11–28	The brothers tested by Joseph as to whether they will protect Benjamin in Egypt; Judah steps forward to offer himself a ransom for Benjamin. Gen. 44:18–34
	Benjamin to dwell between the shoulders of the Lord (Joseph and Judah); beloved of the Lord; will dwell safely. Deut. 33:12		The tribe of Benjamin known to be mighty warriors. 1 Chron. 12:2 Benjamin aligned with Judah. 1 Kings 12:21
			Tribe of Benjamin almost annihilated by the other tribes over the assault on the Levite's concubine. Judg. 19–21
			King Saul from Benjamin

Name/Meaning	Patriarchal Blessing	Land Allotment	Events
Ephraim, "Fruitful" **Sign: Ox**	Birthright son of Joseph; shall become a multitude of nations. Gen. 48:17–20; 1 Chron. 5:1–2	Jordan at Jericho to the waters of Jericho on the east into the wilderness, through the hill country to Bethel, Bethel to Luz, ending at the sea; the holy cities of Shechem and Shiloh were within Ephraim's boundaries; shared with the "western" half of Manasseh. Josh. 16; 17:17	Front (or rear) lines of Israel's safety and defense; brought up the rearward of the camp of Israel; in the front lines in fighting the Canaanites under Joshua (an Ephraimite).
	A future great seer will come through his lineage. JST Gen. 50:24–38		Joshua from Ephraim. Num. 13:8 Samuel the prophet, an Ephraimite. 1 Sam. 1:1
	With horns like a unicorn (or a wild ox) Ephraim will push together the ten thousands of people of the earth (to gather Israel). Deut. 33:13–17		King Jeroboam of Ephraim divided Israel and led them into apostasy. 1 Kings 12:19–20, 25–31; 14:7–12
	The Lord will redeem Ephraim, His "firstborn." Jer. 31:9		Joseph Smith from Ephraim. *Journal of Discourses* 2:268–69
	Ephraim will greet and crown the incoming lost tribes. D&C 133:26–34		

Name/Meaning	Patriarchal Blessing	Land Allotment	Events
	Those who are rebellious will not be counted as "the blood of Ephraim." D&C 64:36		
Manasseh, "Making to Forget" **Sign: Unicorn or Ox**	He will be great but fewer in number than Ephraim. Gen. 48:17–20	Land on both sides of the Jordan (as half-tribe inheritances); included the land of Gilead, some of the richest soil in Israel. Joshua 13:29–31 The land on the western side was shared with Ephraim. Josh. 17:17 (The western side included Mounts Ebal, Gerizim, Gilboa, and Carmel.)	Responded to Hezekiah's invitation to Passover and a healing of Israel after their destruction by Assyria. 2 Chron. 30:11
	Manasseh, with Ephraim, will help gather Israel. Deut. 33:13–17		Gideon from Manasseh. Judges 6:15
			Lehi from Manasseh. Alma 10:3

CHAPTER 3

The Birthright

The idea of a birthright presupposes that the eldest son in a family will receive a double portion of an inheritance upon the death of his father and preside as the priesthood leader over his family, including his mother and siblings. However, according to the scriptural accounts of most families, the birthright rarely follows this pattern.

Although Ishmael was the firstborn son to Abraham and Hagar, Sarah was the first wife, and therefore, her son, Isaac, became the birthright son and inherited those covenant privileges. We have discussed Esau and Jacob in a previous chapter[1] and will now turn to the sons of Jacob, or Israel, and the manner in which Joseph became the birthright son.

In contradiction to the popular play that states that Joseph was given the birthright along with his special coat because his father loved his mother best, we will see that Joseph obtained the birthright because of his own personal righteousness, a standard of faith to which he held even when exiled to a foreign land and cast into prison.

1. See chapter 1 of this publication, "Who Is Israel?"

The Birthright Privilege and Responsibility Modeled after the Firstborn Son of God

In order to fully understand what the blessings of the birthright are, we should fix our eyes upon the Firstborn Son of the Father, Jesus Christ. As the firstborn, who sought ever His Father's will and the means by which to fulfill that will, Jesus earned the full trust and approbation of His Father. He acted in the Father's stead as a faithful steward to the degree that He proclaimed that if one had seen or known Him, he had also seen or known the Father.[2]

As a result of His perfect faithfulness to the Father's will, both in the premortal realm as well as the mortal, Jesus attained Godhood.[3] He formed the earth under the direction of the Father and helped to breathe life into mankind as well. But He was not a distant God who set things in motion and then withdrew to watch the show. Instead, He condescended to set aside the glory and power that came with Godhood in order to dwell among his sisters and brothers and teach, lift, heal, and light a path of truth for them to follow. Bound through love for His siblings and unity with His Father, Jesus offered Himself as a ransom and a sacrifice so that all mankind might be redeemed, healed, and resurrected and brought back into the presence of the Father and the Son throughout eternity.

Although the Father has given everything He has into the hands of His Son as the perfectly obedient Child of His heart, Jesus shares all that He has with His siblings. He makes us joint heirs with Him, sharing absolutely everything He has inherited by right with us.[4] This is the role of the birthright son.

The Birthright and Priesthood

Key to the institution of the birthright is the right of the priesthood, which was passed from father to son with the birthright in ancient times until the restoration of the priesthood in this dispensation

2. John 14:9–11.
3. See Abraham 3.
4. Romans 8:17.

when its blessings are available to all. The Lord explained to Joseph Smith:

> For whoso is faithful unto the obtaining these two priesthoods of which I have spoken [the Aaronic and Melchizedek Priesthoods], and the magnifying their calling [taking their responsibilities seriously in using the priesthood to care for others], are sanctified by the Spirit unto the renewing of their bodies. They become the sons of Moses and of Aaron and the seed of Abraham, and the church and kingdom, and the elect of God. And also all they who receive this priesthood receive me, saith the Lord; For he that receiveth my servants receiveth me; And he that receiveth me receiveth my Father; And he that receiveth my Father receiveth my Father's kingdom; therefore all that my Father hath shall be given unto him. And this is according to the oath and covenant which belongeth to the priesthood.[5]

Abraham was promised that through his priesthood, extending down through the generations and passed from father to son, all of the families of the earth would be blessed.[6] The priesthood is not a responsibility or privilege to pass forward lightly. It is not like a plot of land that goes from hand to hand, but the receiver must qualify for the priesthood through a committed heart and covenant. It was understood that the birthright son, given the priesthood, would take special care of his family: he would see to their needs, including their temporal, spiritual, and emotional welfare, and would share all that he inherited in the way of lands, flocks, and funds—everything under his stewardship. Again, Jesus Christ set the example and standard for the role, and the early mothers and fathers knew about Him and what He would offer as the Messiah from the days of Adam, who was instructed to offer sacrifice in similitude of the Only Begotten of the Father.[7] In fact, the priesthood was originally called after the Order of the Son of God,[8] but was renamed after Melchizedek when that great king used it to bless and sanctify his people, including Father Abraham. Out

5. Doctrine and Covenants 84:33–39.
6. Abraham 2:9–11.
7. Moses 5:6–7.
8. Doctrine and Covenants 107:3.

of "respect or reverence to the name of the Supreme Being, [and] to avoid too frequent repetition of His name, they, the church, in ancient days, called that priesthood after Melchizedek, or the Melchizedek Priesthood."[9] Much about the Melchizedek Priesthood has been lost to scripture, but Paul knew enough about it to acknowledge that it belonged to Jesus Christ and that it needed to be restored to Israel. He wrote to the Hebrews:

> And no man taketh this honor unto himself, but he that is called of God, as was Aaron. So also Christ glorified not himself to be made an high priest; but he that said unto him, Thou art my Son, today have I begotten thee. As he saith also in another place, Thou art a priest forever after the order of Melchizedek.[10]

As Paul noted, no man can take the honor of the priesthood onto himself, regardless of his birth order. If the birthright inheritance were only land and goods, then perhaps the eldest could assert his right, but the weight of responsibility that came with the priesthood was quite another matter, and God would decide that role.

---

9. Doctrine and Covenants 107:4.
10. Hebrews 5:4–6.

CHAPTER 4

Joseph

Some have supposed that because Reuben, Leah's firstborn son, lost the birthright due to his sin against his father and Bilhah, the birthright was then offered to Rachel's firstborn son, Joseph. As we consider the principles discussed in the previous chapter and the weight of responsibility and stewardship that rested upon the birthright son, we may come to see that regardless of birth order, Joseph was destined, and even preordained, to be the birthright son of Israel.

We first meet Joseph when he is seventeen and out feeding the flocks with his elder brothers, Dan, Naphtali, Gad, and Asher.[1] He has brought home "evil reports" concerning them and likely gets them into trouble since he is Jacob's favorite son.

> Now Israel loved Joseph more than all his children, because he was the son of his old age: and he made him a coat of many colours. And when his brethren saw that their father loved him more than all his brethren, they hated him, and could not speak peaceably unto him.[2]

1. Genesis 37:2.
2. Genesis 37:3–4.

The Coat of the Birthright and Priesthood Leadership

What is the coat that caused so much jealousy? The famous play *Joseph and the Amazing Technicolor Dream Coat* says:

> Joseph's coat was elegant, the cut was fine. The tasteful style was the ultimate in good design . . . and when Joseph tried it on, he knew his sheepskin days were gone. Such a dazzling coat of many colors, how he loved his coat of many colors! In a class above the rest, it even went well with his vest. Such a stunning coat of many colors, how he loved his coat of many colors. It was red and yellow and green and brown and blue.

Alfred Edersheim states:

> But in truth it was *not* a "coat of many colours," but a tunic reaching down to the arms and feet, such as princes and persons of distinction wore, and it betokened to Joseph's brothers only too clearly, that their father intended to transfer to Joseph the right of the firstborn.[3]

Matthew Brown adds:

> It was Joseph's investiture with the so-called "coat of many colours" that signaled that he was the birthright son. There are several things that the reader should notice in order to properly understand the nature of Joseph's "coat." First of all, the phrase "coat of many colours" actually comes from the Septuagint, which the Greek translation of the Old Testament made between 284 and 246 BC. This is not what the Hebrew text says, however. The word "many" is not present in the Hebrew text and that is why it has been italicized by the translators of the King James Bible. Hence the phrase should simply read "coat of colours." The next thing to notice about this phrase is that "coat" is translated from the Hebrew work *kuttonet*, and it can mean either garment or robe.[4] This is the very same word used to identify one of the vestments worn by the temple priests of Israel from the time of Moses onward.[5] Indeed, it was understood among later Jewish authors that Joseph's vesture was nothing

3. Alfred Edersheim, *Bible History, Old Testament*, 101–2.
4. *New Strong's Concordance*, 67.
5. See Exodus 28:9.

> less than "the holy tunic of the priest."[6] . . . Interestingly, it is the considered opinion of some biblical interpreters that Joseph's "coat" was not only a "royal garment" but it also signified "the claim of the Joseph tribes to a royal authority independent of the tribe of Judah."[7] The preceding information points to the conclusion that Joseph's distinctive vesture could be seen as both the clothing of a king and a priest. This comes as little surprise when one considers that in Jewish lore the gift that was given by Jacob to Joseph was exactly what he himself had received as part of the birthright blessing, "the garments made by God for Adam."[8]

We have discussed the fact that the birthright held a deep responsibility for honoring and magnifying the priesthood power and stewardship in behalf of others.[9] Recognizing that Joseph's coat was actually a priesthood garment representing priesthood and kingship, we understand why Joseph's owning it would only exacerbate his older brothers' feelings of resentment and jealousy toward him. Why, then, did Joseph tell them his dreams about them bowing down to him? Was it teenage sibling rivalry, or foolish naiveté? What is clear is that young Joseph did not fully realize that the promised bond of gratitude that his family would come to feel for him would come through his own sacrifice and loss.

We have yet another ironic twist to the story in that like Jacob, Joseph would not accumulate his wealth through birthright inheritance (for each went empty-handed from their family homes), but that his promised bounty would come directly from God and through his own effort to work hard and remain true to his faith. Although both Jacob's and Joseph's brothers were angry over what they perceived had been stolen from them, they never lost anything to the birthright son.

---

6. Louis Ginzberg, *The Legend of the Jews*, 5:326–29. According to one writer, the phrase "coat of many colours" should be translated in accordance with Mishnaic materials as "an upper garment in which figures are woven."
7. George Butterick, *The Interpreter's Bible*, 1:749.
8. Louis Ginzberg, *The Legend of the Jews*, 2:139; Matthew B. Brown, *The Gate of Heaven*, 43–44.
9. See chapter 3 of this publication, "The Birthright."

Joseph Is Betrayed by His Brothers

On the day of Joseph's brothers' mutiny against him, Jacob asked Joseph to go and check on them in Shechem, forty-five miles away. Joseph answered like another "Well-Beloved Son," "Here am I," [send me].[10] It is one of many parallels we will observe between Joseph, son of Israel, and Jesus, Son of the Father, who also left home to seek out His brethren.

"And when they saw him afar off, even before he came near unto them, they conspired against him to slay him."[11] Let us note that Reuben, the eldest, and the one with the most to lose if Joseph lived, was the most softhearted among them. He "delivered him out of their hands; and said, Let us not kill him." He suggested that they throw him in a pit, with the intention that he would return later, get Joseph, and deliver him to their father again. He seemed genuinely distressed later when he returned to find that Joseph was gone.[12]

Before they cast him into a dry well, the brothers stripped Joseph of the hated coat. Once again, we note the parallel to the Savior, who was stripped of His garments by the "brothers" who sought His death.[13]

It was Judah's idea that they sell Joseph to the traveling merchants (Ishmaelite cousins) who were on their way to Egypt. They accepted twenty pieces of silver in exchange for their younger brother, the going rate for a slave of his age.[14] Jesus would be sold by Judas (Hebrew: *Judah*) for thirty pieces of silver, the cost of a slave of more mature years.[15] To cover their crime, the brothers tore Joseph's coat, dipped it in the blood of a goat, and took it to their father.[16] Jesus's clothing was likewise stained with His own blood in Gethsemane[17] and by the flogging He received at Pilate's palace.

---

10. Genesis 37:13; Abraham 3:27.
11. Genesis 37:18.
12. Genesis 37:21–22, 29.
13. Genesis 37:23; Luke 23:34.
14. Genesis 37:26–28.
15. Zechariah 11:12; Matthew 26:15.
16. Genesis 37:31–33.
17. Luke 22:44.

Joseph, in Exile, Remains Faithful to His Covenants

Potiphar, Pharaoh's captain of the guard, bought Joseph.[18] Joseph was bereft of family and friends in a strange land. A youth not yet considered a man, how could Joseph maintain his purity and his covenants with God?

Joseph is *the* example of faithfulness under duress. Even when he was in prison, he never exhibited bitterness toward God or man. Much later, when his brothers *did* bow before him in fulfillment of his boyhood dream, Joseph did not gloat but was humble and overcome with tears of joy.[19] He put himself in God's hands, always saw himself as God's instrument, and meekly accepted all that came into his life. We can take great strength from Joseph's example when we encounter our own lonely trials and honor our covenants throughout them.

The Lord *did* bless Joseph for his faithfulness, although not in the ways that most people would look for. "The Lord made all that he did to prosper in his hand,"[20] but he did not release him from Potiphar's employ or keep him from prison under false allegations. In all, Joseph served Potiphar, or was in prison, for a total of thirteen years. Potiphar reaped the blessings of Joseph's goodness, as did the keeper of the prison.[21]

Everyone who met Joseph in Egypt "favored" him,[22] including Potiphar's lascivious wife. Day after day she tried to tempt him, but he would not succumb. His answer to her invitation is recited by seminary students throughout the world: "There is none greater in this house than I; neither hath he kept back anything from me but thee, because thou art his wife: how then can I do this great wickedness, and sin against God?"[23]

Alfred Edersheim adds this interesting insight:

18. Genesis 39:1.
19. Genesis 45:1–8.
20. Genesis 39:3.
21. Genesis 39:5, 23.
22. Genesis 39:21.
23. Genesis 39:9 (a Seminary Scripture Mastery verse).

> We have reason to believe that Potiphar could not in every respect have credited the story of his wife. For the punishment awarded in Egypt to the crime of which she accused him was far more severe than that which Joseph received. Potiphar consigned him to the kings' prison, of which, in his capacity as chief of the body-guard, he was the superintendent.[24]

At long last, Joseph was released from prison to take on his role as Pharoah's most trusted advisor and officer. After interpreting Pharaoh's dream of seven years of plenty, followed by seven years of famine, Pharaoh appointed Joseph to oversee a food storage program that would preserve the lives of thousands.[25] Joseph was second to Pharaoh only in power and authority, but his noble character shone through, because he used his authority with wisdom and honor.[26]

Joseph Saves His Brothers

At least another seven years passed, and Jacob's family was starving in Canaan. He sent all of his sons except Benjamin to Egypt to obtain food. They bowed before Joseph, just as he had dreamed more than twenty years previously.[27] Joseph did not reveal himself to them but rather tested them. Had they matured and changed, or were they the same jealous lot who had sold him away? He accused them of being spies and told them that he would only believe that their goals were pure if they would return with their youngest brother, his own full-blooded sibling, Benjamin. In order to ensure that they would return

---

24. Alfred Edersheim, *Bible History, Old Testament*, 105.
25. Genesis 41:25–41.
26. There is much conjecture about Joseph's impact upon Egyptian government and religion. Some believe that Joseph's Pharaoh was one of the Hyksos, or shepherd-kings, that were hated and later driven out of Egypt. This is presented in the Bible Dictionary as fact. However, archaeologists continue to present various theories, and those theories are constantly changing. While Joseph's role in Egypt is of utmost interest since archeology and history still seek to find a consensus upon which they can agree, this book will only deal with Joseph's role and relationship within the family of Israel.
27. Genesis 42:6.

with Benjamin, Joseph asked that one of the brothers offer himself as a ransom to remain with him until the others returned.[28]

The brothers immediately connected their predicament to the earlier evil they had perpetrated against Joseph. They were full of guilt and anguish over their earlier deeds, and their hearts were fully repentant.[29] They knew that their father had been devastated by Joseph's loss and would not survive losing Benjamin as well. Simeon was taken as ransom, and they worried that he would also be lost. When they returned home to their father, they found that Joseph had returned their money in their sacks, and they feared that they would be accused of theft in addition to all that was already weighing on their heavy hearts.

When their food was once again depleted, Jacob and his sons knew that they must return again to Egypt or starve. They were terrified of Joseph, and for Benjamin. They didn't know why Joseph had asked this thing of them: that they must bring their younger brother with them or they could not have food. Jacob was beside himself with fear and worry. Both Reuben and Judah offered themselves as surety for Benjamin's safety.[30] Their offers provide proof of the change they had undergone since they sold Joseph as a slave.

When Joseph saw his brothers return with Benjamin, he had to find a secret place in which to weep. He was overcome at seeing his younger brother. But he was not through testing his brothers' integrity. He told his servants to return the money yet again to his brothers' sacks and also to plant his own cup in Benjamin's bag. After they departed, he sent his servants after them, claiming that a cup had been stolen. The brothers were horrified and agreed to Joseph's terms that if the cup was found, the person who had it would be bound to him as a slave. When the cup was found in Benjamin's belongings, the brothers tore their clothes in an agony of grief. Judah threw himself before Joseph and pleaded that Joseph would take *him*, Judah, as a slave in Benjamin's place.[31]

---

28. Genesis 42:8–20.

29. Genesis 42:21–22.

30. Genesis 42:37; 43:8–9.

31. Genesis 44.

When Joseph heard Judah's words and recognized their sincerity, he "wept aloud" and revealed himself to them all. "I am Joseph your brother, whom ye sold into Egypt."[32]

No angry words did Joseph utter, but he reassured his brothers that what had happened to him had been orchestrated by God. What Joseph shared with his brothers about his purpose continues down through the generations as the purpose of Joseph's descendants:

> Now therefore be not grieved, nor angry with yourself, that ye sold me hither: for God did send me before you to preserve life. . . . And God sent me before you to preserve you a posterity in the earth, and to save your lives by a great deliverance. So now it was not you that sent me hither, but God . . . ye thought evil against me; but God meant it unto good, to bring to pass, as it is this day, to save much people alive.[33]

The Legacy of Joseph and of Judah

Joseph's heritage and legacy to save Israel and preserve life is still in effect today, which we shall see as we trace his lineage through the ages and discuss the sacred commission that many of his bloodline have received to go forward in the work that Joseph began.

As we proceed, we will also see the unique bond between Joseph and Judah that began with the brothers and continues through time. Judah initially sold Joseph, and while his act was performed out of spite, it also was an attempt to save Joseph's life from the more bloodthirsty members of the family. Twenty years later, it was Judah who offered himself as a ransom for Benjamin, having had his heart pricked, broken, and repentant of the deed performed in his youth. These two—Joseph and Judah—will have their names linked throughout the history and the future of Israel. They are the two leaders of Israel who must come together once again to bring the tribes to unity and life.

There are many similarities in Joseph's life to that of Jesus Christ, the Messiah. Joseph's life foreshadowed the Savior's in the following ways:

---

32. Genesis 45:1–4.
33. Genesis 45:5–8; 50:20.

Joseph	Jesus Christ
The birthright son, exercising stewardship and salvation for his family.	The birthright Son, exercising stewardship and salvation for His family.
When Jacob called for him to go to Shechem, Joseph answered, "Here am I" (Gen. 37:13).	When called to fulfill the Plan of Salvation, Jesus answered, "Here am I. Send Me" (Abraham 3:27).
Joseph's brothers stripped him of his coat (Gen. 37:23).	Jesus was stripped of His garments by the "brothers" who sought His death (Luke 23:34).
Joseph's brothers covered his coat in blood (Gen. 37:31).	Jesus's garment was covered in His blood (Luke 22:44).
Sold by his brother Judah for a price of a slave (Gen. 37:26–28).	Sold by Judas (Hebrew: *Judah*) for the price of a slave (Zech. 11:12; Matt. 26:15).
Began his ministry under Pharaoh at thirty years old (Gen. 41:46).	Began his public ministry at thirty years old.
Everyone from all countries came to Joseph for bread (Gen. 41:5–57).	Everyone must come to Jesus Christ for the bread and water of life (John 6–7).

CHAPTER 5

Judah

Judah and Tamar

The first account we have of Judah as an individual is recorded in Genesis 38. We learn that he had three sons by a Canaanite woman, indicating that he had married outside of the covenant. His oldest son, Er, had married a woman named Tamar, but Er was so wicked that the Lord struck him down.[1] When Er died, Judah gave Tamar to his next oldest son, Onan, who was also wicked and also killed by the Lord.[2]

Judah seemed to connect the deaths of his sons to Tamar, for when by Levirate law[3] he should have wed Tamar to his third son, Shelah, he delayed the marriage and told her to remain a widow in her father's home, taking no responsibility for her as a member of his own family.[4]

Some years later, and after the death of Judah's wife, Tamar, frustrated over her ongoing widowhood, dressed herself as a harlot and sat

1. Genesis 38:1–7.
2. Genesis 38:8–10.
3. Levirate marriage requires the brother of a dead man to marry his brother's wife and bring up a son under the name of the dead brother that he might have posterity.
4. Genesis 38:11.

on the side of the road, waiting for Judah on his way to shear his sheep. Not recognizing Tamar as his own daughter-in-law, Judah engaged her services, with a pledge payment of his own signet, bracelets, and staff.[5]

About three months later, word was brought to Judah that his daughter-in-law was pregnant, and therefore had clearly been immoral. Judah, who had neglected Tamar as a member of his household and family, now, in indignation, declared that she should be brought to him so that he could see her put to death by fire.[6] When Tamar came before Judah, she presented the signet ring, the bracelets, and the staff and said, "These belong to the man who is the father of my child."[7]

Judah acknowledged the fact that Tamar had been more righteous than he in that he had not done right by her on many counts. He also acknowledged her twin sons as his. Through their son Pharez came Boaz, and later, Jesus Christ.[8] Tamar is specifically mentioned in Jesus's genealogy.[9]

Judah's Legacy and Responsibility

Judah's response to Tamar, as well as his offer to give himself as a ransom for Benjamin's life,[10] seems to illustrate that while quick-tempered, Judah was also quick to accept responsibility for his actions and to seek repentance and reconciliation.

We know very little about Judah the man from the accounts that remain in the scriptures; however, based upon the significant patriarchal blessing pronounced upon him by his father, Jacob, or Israel, the Lord acknowledges Judah as being set apart and worthy to have kings and the Messiah come through his lineage.[11]

---

5. Genesis 38:13–18.
6. Genesis 38:24.
7. Genesis 38:25.
8. Ruth 4:18–22; Luke 3:23–38.
9. Matthew 1:3.
10. Genesis 44:33.
11. See Genesis 49:8–12.

CHAPTER 6

The Patriarchal Blessings of Judah and Joseph

Judah and Joseph Assigned Leadership in Israel

THE PATRIARCHAL BLESSINGS GIVEN TO JUDAH AND JOSEPH STAND out from their brothers'. Despite their expectations surrounding birth order and birthright, the Lord reveals His will and plan for each of the brothers and their tribes, and both Joseph and Judah receive blessings and prophecies of leadership: to Judah, an emphasis on kingship, and to Joseph, we might see a focus on the priesthood aspect of leadership that comes with the birthright. Both are told that their siblings will bow down to them. Both carry the weight of responsibility for Israel. And, as we shall see, these blessings are not intended for the individual brother alone, but for their posterity as well, a legacy of leadership that is in effect through to the end of time and into the millennial reign of the Messiah ben Judah.[1]

1. Father Jacob, or Israel, stated, "Gather yourselves together, that I may tell you that which shall befall you in the last days" (Genesis 49:1).

Judah's Blessing

The blessing that Jacob, Israel, pronounced on his son, Judah, is as follows:

> Judah, thou art he whom thy brethren shall praise: thy hand shall be in the neck of thine enemies; thy father's children shall bow down before thee. Judah is a lion's whelp: from the prey, my son, thou art gone up: he stooped down, he couched as a lion, and as an old lion; who shall rouse him up?
>
> The scepter shall not depart from Judah, nor a lawgiver from between his feet, until Shiloh come; and unto him shall the gathering of the people be.
>
> Binding his foal unto the vine, and his ass's colt unto the choice vine; he washed his garments in wine, and his clothes in the blood of grapes: His eyes shall be red with wine, and his teeth white with milk.[2]

Alfred Edersheim comments:

> The three older brothers being dispossessed, and Joseph receiving the twofold territorial portion, the other privileges of the birthright are solemnly transferred to Judah. He is to be the leader, "the lion." As the lion is king of the forest, so was Judah to have royal sway, through David onwards to the Son of David, the *Shiloh*, unto Whom, as "the Lion of the tribe of Judah," all nations should render homage and obedience. Similarly, fulness of earthly riches was to distinguish the lot of Judah, these earthly blessings being themselves emblems of the spiritual riches dispensed in the portion of Judah. The whole description here is full of Messianic allusions, which were afterwards taken up in the prophecy of Balaam;[3] then applied to David;[4] and from him carried forward in prophecy, through till they were finally realized in Jesus Christ, "sprung out of Judah."[5, 6]

---

2. Genesis 49:8–12.
3. Numbers 23:24; 24:9, 17.
4. Psalm 89:20–37.
5. Hebrews 7:14; see Psalm 72; Isaiah 9, 11; Ezekiel 21:27; Zechariah 9:9.
6. Alfred Edersheim, *Bible History, Old Testament*, 127–28.

Kings and the Messiah to Come through Judah

Jeffrey M. Bradshaw shares some of the interpretations that have been offered regarding Judah's blessing:

> Themes of kingship in Judah's blessings also have application to the coming of the Messiah through his lineage—for example, the call for "praise" of Judah (a term generally reserved for God Himself), allusions to the metaphoric "lion of Judah"—a name of Christ, the title "Shiloh"—another name for the Messiah, and the imagery of king appareled in a red robe washed as if in "blood."[7]

Bradshaw continues in breaking down possible interpretations:

> *Judah is a lion's whelp*—the young lion is "a metaphor of strength, daring, and unassailability"[8] The lion became a favorite symbol in later Jewish art and literature.
>
> *He crouches down, he stretches out like a lion, like a lioness—who dares rouse him up*? Judah is pictured "like a lion that seizes its prey, returns to its den, and dares anyone to challenge it . . . This image foreshadows the military triumphs of David and gave rise to the Messianic title "The Lion of Judah."[9]
>
> *The scepter shall not depart from Judah . . . until tribute comes to him; and the obedience of peoples is his.* This prophecy is fulfilled both in the kingship of David and also that of Christ, the "Son of David."
>
> *Until Shiloh come and unto him shall the gathering of the people be.* Note that JST Genesis 50:24 asserts in a parenthetical aside that "Messiah . . . is called Shiloh."[10] The footnote for Genesis 49:10,

---

7. Jeffrey M. Bradshaw, "How Should We Understand the Symbolism in Jacob's Blessing of Judah and Joseph?"
8. N. M. Sarna (336), as quoted by Jeffrey M. Bradshaw in "How Should We Understand the Symbolism in Jacob's Blessing of Judah and Joseph?"
9. G. J. Wenham (Genesis 49:8), as quoted by Jeffrey M. Bradshaw in "How Should We Understand the Symbolism in Jacob's Blessing of Judah and Joseph?"
10. Jeffrey M. Bradshaw, "How Should We Understand the Symbolism in Jacob's Blessing of Judah and Joseph?"

where Shiloh is written, states, "The Hebrew word *shiloh* may be a short form of *asher-lo,* which can be rendered 'whose right it is.'"

Binding his foal to the vine . . . he washes his garments in wine. The medieval Jewish scholar Ibn Ezra explained the gist of this verse with clarity: "The yield of his vineyards will be so abundant that his ass can turn aside to the vine and he won't care if it eats the grapes." This explanation jibes nicely with the next image of washing garments in wine—the wine will be so plentiful that it can be treated as water.[11]

His robe in the blood of grapes. This phrase may refer to the "stained garments of those engaged in the manufacture of wine."[12] A poetical reference to the same idea is found in Isaiah 63 as part of a messianic passage. Ancient readers would have recognized the connection between "blood of grapes," and the blood of the people "trampled in my fury" and "sprinkled upon my garments." They would have also recognized red as a symbol of the "glorious . . . apparel" of kings.[13]

Judah's blessing is glorious, indeed, and eventually led to the tribes of Israel uniting themselves, for a time, under Judah's banner. However, as the writer of Chronicles states, *"For Judah prevailed above his brethren, and of him came the chief ruler; but the birthright was Joseph's."*[14]

Joseph's Blessing

Jacob's blessing to Joseph, and through Joseph to Ephraim and Manasseh, was also full of promise. Jeffrey M. Bradshaw wrote:

---

11. R. Alter (296), as quoted by Jeffrey M. Bradshaw in "How Should We Understand the Symbolism in Jacob's Blessing of Judah and Joseph?"
12. N. M. Sarna (Genesis 49:11), as quoted by Jeffrey M. Bradshaw in "How Should We Understand the Symbolism in Jacob's Blessing of Judah and Joseph?"
13. J. H. Walton (Genesis 49:11), as quoted by Jeffrey M. Bradshaw in "How Should We Understand the Symbolism in Jacob's Blessing of Judah and Joseph?"
14. 1 Chronicles 5:2.

> Although at least one verse is devoted to each of the twelve sons of Jacob, the blessings of Judah and Joseph—the progenitors of the dominant tribes of the later southern and northern kingdoms—are of special significance. "The testament to Joseph is of extraordinary length, equaled only, and significantly, by that to Judah. Lavish blessing is showered upon Joseph, the name here standing for Ephraim and Manasseh together."[15] [Note Bradshaw's confirmation that Ephraim, Manasseh, and Joseph are treated as *one*.]

The following record of Jacob's blessing to Joseph will include edits and additions from the Joseph Smith Translation of the Bible:

> Joseph is a fruitful bough, even a fruitful bough by a well; whose branches run over the wall:
>
> The archers have sorely grieved him, and shot at him, and hated him: But his bow abode in strength, and the arms of his hands were made strong by the hands of the mighty God of Jacob; (from thence is the shepherd, the stone of Israel:)
>
> Even by the God of thy father, who shall help thee; and by the Almighty, who shall bless thee with blessings of heaven above, blessings of the deep that lieth under, blessings of the breasts, and of the womb:
>
> The blessings of thy father have prevailed above the blessings of my progenitors unto the utmost bound of the everlasting hills: they shall be on the head of Joseph, and on the crown of the head of him that was separate from his brethren.[16]

Fruitful Branches from Joseph's Lineage

The first promise of Joseph's blessing refers to a *fruitful bough by a well*, or fed continuously by a spring of water, *whose branches run over the wall.* Just before his death, Joseph told his people some of

---

15. N. M. Sarna (342), as quoted by Jeffrey M. Bradshaw in "How Should We Understand the Symbolism in Jacob's Blessing of Judah and Joseph?"
16. Genesis 49:22–26.

what would befall them in the coming centuries. Referring to his own patriarchal blessing and his own lineage, Joseph prophesied, "*And it shall come to pass that they shall be scattered again; and a branch shall be broken off, and shall be carried into a far country; nevertheless they shall be remembered in the covenants of the Lord . . .*"[17]

Considering the fact that Joseph's lineage were the first to be taken captive and scattered by the Assyrians in 721 BC, there have undoubtedly been many dispersions of Joseph's posterity in fulfillment of his patriarchal blessing. Their records are yet to be known.

However, we know of one particular family who made their way to the New World at the time of the Babylonian captivity of Jerusalem (587 BC) and kept their records in what we now call the Book of Mormon. Lehi, the prophet who led this expedition, taught his sons:

> For behold, thou art the fruit of my loins; and I am a descendant of Joseph who was carried captive into Egypt. And great were the covenants of the Lord which he made unto Joseph. Wherefore, Joseph truly saw our day. And he obtained a promise of the Lord, that out of the fruit of his loins the Lord God would raise up a righteous branch unto the house of Israel; not the Messiah, but a branch which was to be broken off, nevertheless, to be remembered in the covenants of the Lord that the Messiah should be made manifest unto them in the latter days, in the spirit of power, unto the bringing of them out of darkness unto light—yea, out of hidden darkness and out of captivity unto freedom.[18]

Lehi's son, Nephi, told his people:

> Behold, I say unto you, that the house of Israel was compared unto an olive tree, by the Spirit of the Lord which was in our father; and behold are we not broken off from the house of Israel, and are we not a branch of the house of Israel? Behold, I say unto you, Yea; they shall be remembered again among the house of Israel; they shall be grafted in, being a natural branch of the olive tree, into the true olive tree.[19]

---

17. Genesis 50:25, Joseph Smith Translation.
18. 2 Nephi 3:4–5.
19. 1 Nephi 15:12, 16; see 1 Nephi 19:24.

The prophet Jacob, also a son of Lehi, added, "Wherefore, thus saith the Lord, I have led this people forth out of the land of Jerusalem, by the power of mine arm, that I might raise up unto me a righteous branch from the fruit of the loins of Joseph."[20]

Blessings of Abundance through the Birthright

Jacob's blessing to Joseph continues: *The archers have sorely grieved him, and shot at him, and hated him: But his bow abode in strength, and the arms of his hands were made strong by the hands of the mighty God of Jacob; (from thence is the shepherd, the stone of Israel:).* Although for a time it looked as if Joseph was lost and divided from his family, the Lord made him strong and fulfilled the blessings of the birthright upon him. He obtained a position of honor and power in Egypt whereby he was able to deliver and save Israel. God chose and strengthened Joseph. The Shepherd and Stone of Israel, the Messiah,[21] used, and is still using, Joseph and his descendants in His work.

Even by the God of thy father, who shall help thee; and by the Almighty, who shall bless thee with blessings of heaven above, blessings of the deep that lieth under, blessings of the breasts, and of the womb: Joseph is promised the help of God and blessings of abundance that include the blessing of posterity.

The blessings of thy father have prevailed above the blessings of my progenitors unto the utmost bound of the everlasting hills: they shall be on the head of Joseph, and on the crown of the head of him that was separate from his brethren: the blessings of Jacob and of Joseph will be even greater than those that went before them (Abraham and Isaac), even unto the utmost bounds of the ends of the earth.

Responsibilities of the Tribe of Joseph

The Joseph Smith Translation of the Bible adds the following to Jacob's blessing of Joseph:

20. Jacob 2:25.
21. Doctrine and Covenants 50:44.

> When the God of my fathers appeared unto me in Luz, in the land of Canaan; he sware unto me, that he would give unto me, and unto my seed, the land for an everlasting possession.
>
> Therefore, O my son, he hath blessed me in raising thee up to be a servant unto me, in saving my house from death; In delivering my people, thy brethren, from famine which was sore in the land; wherefore the God of thy fathers shall bless thee, and the fruit of thy loins, that they shall be blessed above thy brethren, and above thy father's house.

Joseph (and through Joseph, Ephraim and Manasseh) receive the greatest blessings of all of the house of Israel. But with those blessings will come great responsibility.

> For thou hast prevailed, and thy father's house hath bowed down unto thee, even as it was shown unto thee, before thou wast sold into Egypt by the hands of thy brethren; wherefore thy brethren shall bow down unto thee, from generation to generation, unto the fruit of thy loins forever; For thou shalt be a light unto my people, to deliver them in the days of their captivity, from bondage; and to bring salvation unto them, when they are altogether bowed down under sin.[22]

Even as Joseph was separated from his family in order to do them good in providing food for them in Egypt, so shall Joseph's lineage continue to provide salvation and light to the house of Israel.

The blessings Jacob gave to Ephraim and Manasseh through Joseph promised that both would become great in the number of their posterity, but that Ephraim would be greater, "and his seed shall become a multitude of nations."[23] The Joseph Smith Translation of the Bible adds that Jacob "adopted" Ephraim and Manasseh into his family, and they were to be known and called after the house of Israel.[24]

---

22. Genesis 48:5–11, Joseph Smith Translation.
23. Genesis 48:17–20
24. Genesis 48:5, Joseph Smith Translation.

Messiah ben Judah (David) and Messiah ben Joseph

The blessings on Judah and Joseph were so great that they gave rise to the belief that there would actually be *two* Messiahs: Messiah ben Judah (or David), and Messiah ben Joseph (Messiah, son of Judah or David, and Messiah, son of Joseph).

The prophecies regarding Messiah ben Judah, or Messiah ben David, are fulfilled in the person of Yeshua, or Jesus, the Christ. As prophesied in Judah's blessing, the Messiah would come from his loins. The promise was confirmed through King David, who, when he wanted to build a temple for God, was told that the Messiah, Son of God, would come through his posterity.[25] These important prophecies reveal why it was that Herod's advisors were quick to remember that the Messiah would be born in Bethlehem (David's birthplace)[26] and that when people accepted Jesus as that Messiah, they referred to Him as "the Son of David."[27]

But what of the Messiah ben Yossef, or Messiah, son of Joseph? Rabbi Immanuel Schochet explains:

> Jewish tradition speaks of two redeemers, each one called Mashiach (Messiah). Both are involved in ushering in the Messianic era. They are Mashiach ben David and Mashiach ben Yossef.[28]
>
> The term Mashiach unqualified always refers to Mashiach ben David (Mashiach the descendant of David) of the tribe of Judah. He is the actual (final) redeemer who shall rule in the Messianic age. All that was said in our text relates to him.
>
> Mashiach ben Yossef (Mashiach the descendant of Joseph) of the tribe of Ephraim (son of Joseph) is also referred to as Mashiah ben

25. See 2 Samuel 7:12–15; Isaiah 11:1; Jeremiah 23:5–6.
26. Matthew 2:4–6.
27. Matthew 1:1; 9:27; 12:23; and others.
28. See *Sukah* 52b; *Zohar* 1:25b, II:120a, III:153b, 246b, and 252a; and *Sha'arei Zohar* on *Sukah* 52a for further relevant sources in the *Zohar* writings.

> Ephrayim, Mashiach the descendant of Ephraim.[29] He will come first, before the final redeemer, and later will serve as his viceroy.[30]
>
> The essential task of Mashiach ben Yossef is to act as precursor to Mashiach ben David: he will prepare the world for the coming of the final redeemer. Different sources attribute to him different functions, some even charging him with tasks traditionally associated with Mashiach ben David (such as the ingathering of the exiles, the rebuilding of the *Bet Hamikdash* [the temple], and so forth).[31]
>
> . . . The essential function of Mashiach ben Yossef is to prepare Israel for the final redemption, to put them into the proper condition in order to clear the way for Mashiach ben David to come. Of that ultimate redemption it is said, that if Israel repent (return to G-d) they shall be redeemed immediately (even before the predetermined date for Mashiach's coming). . . .[32]

The hope and longing for the two Messiahs, each with a vital role, represent the deep connection between Judah and Joseph, a connection that is still essential today. We shall see that the hope that a Messiah, son of Joseph or Ephraim, would prepare the way for the *second* coming of the Messiah, son of Judah or David, is being fulfilled in our time. The promises made to Judah and Joseph are still in effect, and we as their children have the opportunity to inherit the blessings and the duties of our forefathers (and mothers).

---

29. *Sukah* 52 a–b; *Zohar* 1:25b, III:246b, 252b, and others; and *Midrash Agadat Mashiach* use the term Mashiach ben Yossef.
30. The harmony and cooperation between Mashiach ben David and Mashiach ben Yossef signifies the total unity of Israel, removing the historical rivalries between the tribes of Judah and Joseph; see Isaiah 11:13 and Rashi (Rabbi Shlomo Yitzchaki [1040–1105]). Compare *Bereishit Rabba* 70:15 and *Torah Shelemah* on Genesis 29:16, note 49.
31. See *Pirkei Heichalot Rabatt*, ch. 39; *Sefer Zerubavel*; *Midrash Agadat Mashiach* (most of which is quoted in *Leach Tov*, Balak, on Numbers 24:17); compare Rashi (Rabbi Shlomo Yitzchaki [1040–1105]) on *Sukah* 52b; see *Charashim*. See also Ramban, *Commentary on Song* 8:13.
32. Immanuel Schochet, "Mashiach ben Yossef," chabad.org.

CHAPTER 7

Moses and the Camp of Israel

Promises to the Fathers

THE ISRAELITES SPENT FOUR HUNDRED YEARS IN EGYPT, JUST AS THE Lord had foretold Abraham that they would. Even as God was promising a numberless posterity to Abraham, He said:

> Know of a surety that thy seed shall be a stranger in a land that is not theirs, and shall serve them; and they shall afflict them four hundred years; And also that nation, whom they shall serve, will I judge: and afterward shall they come out with great substance.[1]

Were the Israelites familiar with the prophecy? Was Joseph? Before his death, Joseph foresaw that eventual bondage of his people:

> Joseph said unto his brethren, I die, and go unto my fathers; and I go down to my grave with joy. The God of my father Jacob be with you, to deliver you out of affliction in the days of your bondage; for the Lord hath visited me, and I have obtained a promise of the Lord . . . [that] the Lord God will raise up . . . a prophet; (not

1. Genesis 15:13.

> the Messiah who is called Shilo;) and this prophet shall deliver my people out of Egypt in the days of thy bondage.[2]

Joseph received further detail regarding that prophet from the Lord:

> For a seer will I raise up to deliver my people out of the land of Egypt; and he shall be called Moses. And by this name he shall know that he is of thy house [the house of Israel]; for he shall be nursed by the kings' daughter, and shall be called her son.[3]

The clarity and detail of this prophecy (among many others) have caused some to doubt and accuse later writers of recording it after the fact. But the Lord asked through the prophet Isaiah, "Have ye not known? Have ye not heard? Hath it not been told you from the beginning? Have ye not understood from the foundations of the earth?"[4] Indeed, the Lord has foretold much so that we are not only prepared and full of hopeful faith but also so we do not give credit elsewhere when His words come to pass.

> And the Lord sware unto Joseph that he would preserve his seed forever, saying, I will raise up Moses, and a rod shall be in his hand, and he shall gather together my people, and he shall lead them as a flock, and he shall smite the waters of the Red Sea with his rod. And he shall have judgment, and shall write the word of the Lord. And he shall not speak many words, for I will write unto him my law by the finger of mine own hand. And I will make a spokesman for him, and his name shall be called Aaron.
>
> . . . Therefore, Joseph said unto his brethren, God will surely visit you, and bring you out of this land, unto the land which he sware unto Abraham, and unto Isaac, and to Jacob.[5]

How much knowledge had the Israelites retained of their covenant family and the promises made to Abraham, Isaac, Jacob, and Joseph? Did they know of the prophecy of four hundred years in Egypt? Had

---

2. Genesis 50:24, Joseph Smith Translation.
3. Genesis 50:29, Joseph Smith Translation.
4. Isaiah 40:21.
5. Genesis 50:34–36, Joseph Smith Translation.

they retained hope, or had they become assimilated in the culture that surrounded them?

Regardless of whether or not the Israelites remembered, God remembered *them*:

> And the children of Israel sighed by reason of the bondage, and they cried, and their cry came up unto God by reason of the bondage. And God heard their groaning, and God remembered his covenant with Abraham, with Isaac, and with Jacob. And God looked upon the children of Israel, and God had respect unto them.[6]

The Birth of Israel as a Nation and a Covenant People

The Israelites did not at first know whether they could trust Moses. Deliverance—and faith—did not come immediately. The burdens became even greater for the children of Israel after Moses and Aaron spoke to Pharaoh.[7] Because of their painful circumstances, the Israelites were uncertain about Moses's role and concerned that he stirred the Pharaoh up in anger against them. They, like Pharaoh, did not believe that the Lord had power to deliver them.[8]

God had referred to Israel as His own firstborn son,[9] and Israel was about to be born anew as a nation and as a covenant people as they passed through their bloody Passover doorposts, walked through the waters of the Red Sea on dry ground, and experienced the fiery pillar of the Lord as He led them to Mount Sinai. We are born again through blood, water, and the "fire" of the Spirit,[10] and all of these symbols were present as Israel, the "firstborn" nation unto God, was being called out of Egypt to finally inherit the land promised to Abraham and Sarah.[11]

As we see the prophecies being fulfilled with such perfection, we can take comfort in the many promises that are still evolving in their fulfillment, including those given to all of the mothers and fathers

---

6. Exodus 2:23–25.
7. Exodus 5:7–19.
8. Exodus 5:2; 6:9.
9. Exodus 4:22–23.
10. Moses 6:59.
11. See Lynda Cherry, *The Feasts and Festivals of the Messiah*, chapter 7.

who have preceded us. God has not forgotten or forsaken us. Even when we feel as if we are in bondage in a foreign land, a place not of our choosing, we can trust that He does hear our cries and will lead us in His own time to our promised lands. The promises are real, and we can play a part in their fulfillment as we heed the call of the Lord.

The Tribe of Levi and the Call to the Priesthood

With the Lord's call to Moses and Aaron, we also see a call to the tribe of Levi in what becomes their sacred stewardship for the temple and the Levitical, or Aaronic, Priesthood. Whereas the Lord had initially asked that the firstborn son of every family be consecrated (set apart) to Him in remembrance of the fact that it was the death of the firstborn that had freed Israel from bondage, He instructed Moses that the Levites were to become "His" in their stead.[12] The Levites, then, became proxy for the people before the Lord, and symbolically, they also became a proxy for the Messiah/High Priest who would carry the people on His heart (as represented by the breastplate with its twelve stones) into the Holy of Holies. As we read the Lord's instructions about the firstborn belonging to Him, we recognize the symbolic relationship to God's own Firstborn Son: "All the firstborn are mine; for on the day that I smote all the first born in the land of Egypt I hallowed unto me all the firstborn in Israel, both man and beast: mine shall they be: I am the Lord."[13] God's Firstborn Son would be sacrificed and give His life in order to save covenant Israel, and this was represented by all that would take place within the tabernacle temple.

While we don't know how or if the individual tribes maintained their identity in Egypt, the nation of Israel was born anew at Mount Sinai, and tribal identities were noted and given specific responsibilities by Moses as instructed by the Lord. This is particularly notable in the arrangement of the camp of Israel where tribes were assigned specific locations surrounding the tabernacle. The Levites' place was in the midst of the camp, near the tabernacle, for which they had every care.[14]

---

12. Numbers 3:12–13.
13. Numbers 3:12.
14. Numbers 2:17.

TRIBAL IDENTITIES and RESPONSIBILITIES within the CAMP of ISRAEL

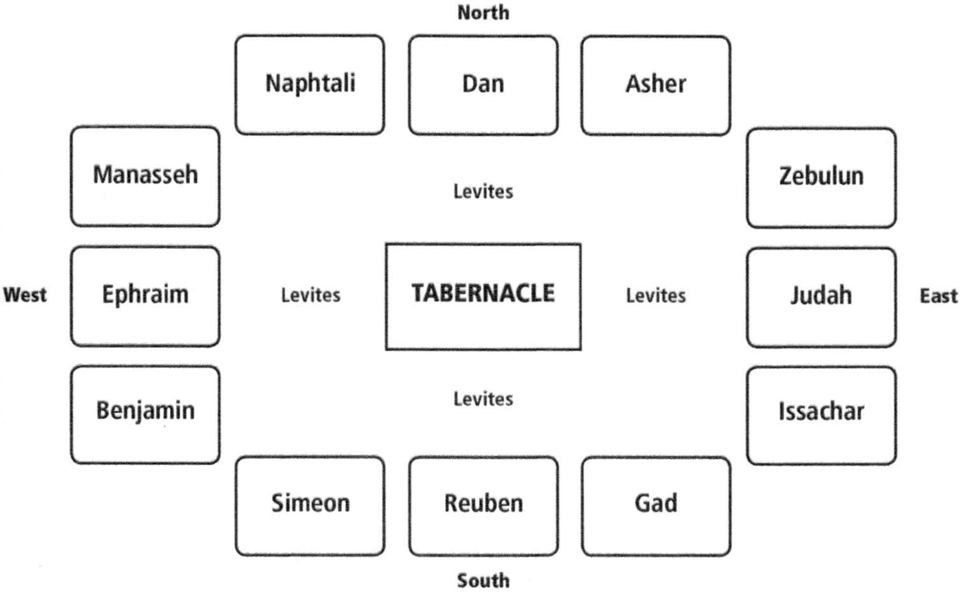

The Lord instructed Moses that each tribe should erect a standard or ensign for identification.[15] Facing east, toward the rising sun, the tribe of Judah held the front position of the camp, with Issachar and Zebulun accompanying Judah. On the south side stood the tribe of Reuben, with Simeon and Gad. The west side, or the rear, was led by the tribe of Ephraim, with Manasseh and Benjamin. The north was held by Dan, accompanied by Asher and Naphtali.[16]

The most dangerous positions were those captained by Judah, who led the forward movement of the camp, and Ephraim, who brought up the rearguard. We see in these arrangements the recognition of the leadership role of these two tribes and the fact that Ephraim and Manasseh have taken their position as "the tribe of Joseph." We will rarely see Joseph's tribe referred to by any name other than "Ephraim and Manasseh" in the future.

---

15. Numbers 2:2.
16. Numbers 2:3–31.

It's interesting to note that Ezekiel's unique vision describing a creature with four faces that were 1) a man, 2) a lion, 3) an ox, and 4) an eagle[17] could be describing the banners of the tribes who guarded the four sides of the camp of Israel. Reuben's ensign is a man, Judah's a lion, Ephraim's an ox, and Dan's an eagle.[18]

John, in his revelation, also saw four "beasts" near the throne of God, 1) a man, 2) a lion, 3) an ox, and 4) an eagle.[19] Both Ezekiel and John describe the creatures they see as having wings, knowledge, and being full of glory. While Ezekiel's vision is more opaque to our understanding, John's focuses on all the creations of God who are sanctified and exalted in His Kingdom.[20] In other parts of his vision, John records an infinite number of each of the tribes of Israel as having attained salvation,[21] and he sees the name of each tribe on the twelve gates of the celestial city.[22] In that context, perhaps the four faces are representative of all of the tribes of Israel and their place within God's Kingdom.

Just before his final farewell to the Israelites, and before they crossed into the long-hoped-for promised land, Moses gave his last warnings and instructions and also his last blessings upon the tribes. Moses told them:

> When the most High divided the nations their inheritance, when he separated the sons of Adam, he set the bounds of the people according to the number of the children of Israel. For the Lord's portion is his people; Jacob [Israel] is the lot of his inheritance. He found him in a desert land, and in the waste howling wilderness; he led him about, he instructed him, he kept him as the apple of his eye.[23]

---

17. Ezekiel 1:1–10.
18. See chapter 2 of this publication, "Twelve Sons, Twelve Tribes" for a chart of all of the tribes and their ensigns.
19. Revelation 4:6–8.
20. See Doctrine and Covenants 77.
21. Revelation 7:4–12.
22. Revelation 21:12.
23. Deuteronomy 32:8–10.

Moses gave each tribe his blessing, and in keeping with our focus on Judah and Joseph, we will turn our attention to Moses's prophecies regarding them, as well as to the blessing given to Levi, now raised up because of the sacred temple duties the tribe had been assigned.

Moses's Blessing on the Tribe of Judah

> And this is the blessing of Judah: and he said, Hear, Lord, the voice of Judah, and bring him unto his people: let his hands be sufficient for him; and be thou an help to him from his enemies.[24]

The plea to the Lord to *"hear the voice of Judah, and bring him unto his people"* surely has fulfillment on many time lines. The tribe of Judah (the Jews) were delivered from the conquering Assyrian army under King Hezekiah and the prophet Isaiah.[25] However, they were not saved from Babylon's conquering forces.[26]

While in the courts of Babylon, Daniel, of the royal house of Judah, fasted and prayed and reminded his people to have faith in the Lord's promise that their freedom from Babylon would come after seventy years, which indeed did occur according to prophecy.[27]

The Jews were allowed to return to their homeland and to build a temple, but later, once again, they became a conquered people under the Greeks and Romans. They prayed for a deliverance that did not come in the way they had hoped for and anticipated. Instead, Jesus Christ, of the tribe of Judah, Messiah ben David, was born and ministered among them and performed an Atonement that offered an eternal salvation and deliverance.

Later, in AD 70, Judah was again vanquished and dispersed, and they have experienced terrible suffering throughout the ages. They have pled for hope and for a return of their promised blessings and promised lands.

---

24. Deuteronomy 33:7.
25. See Isaiah 37.
26. See Jeremiah 39; 2 Chronicles 36:5–20.
27. See Daniel 9:2; Ezra 1–2; Nehemiah 2; 2 Chronicles 36:23.

Now, in our dispensation, Joseph Smith has joined his cries with theirs, and in the first temple of this dispensation, prayed that Judah might return to their promised lands.[28]

Moses's Blessing on the Tribe of Levi

Levi's original "blessing" from Father Jacob had been harsh and reverberated like a curse due to Levi's and Simeon's murder of a city full of people. Now, after centuries, the tribe of Levi had brought forth both Moses and Aaron and a generation who honored the covenants of the Lord.

Moses pronounced this blessing on Levi:

> And of Levi . . . Let thy Thummim and thy Urim be with the holy one, whom thou didst prove at Massah, and with whom thou didst strive at the waters of Meribah; Who said unto his father and to his mother, I have not seen him; neither did he acknowledge his brethren, nor knew his own children: for they have observed thy word, and kept thy covenant. They shall teach Jacob [Israel] thy judgments [Hebrew: ordinances], and Israel thy law: they shall put incense before thee, and whole burnt sacrifice upon thine altar. Bless, Lord, his substance, and accept the work of his hands: smite through the loins of them that rise against him, and of them that hate him, that they rise not again.[29]

It was quite a responsibility to care for the sacred furnishings and ordinances of the temple. This was a blessing carried down through the tribe to righteous Zacharias and his son, John the Baptist.[30] With the destruction of the temple in AD 70, the work of the Levites stopped. We are promised that the tribe of Levi will "offer again an offering in righteousness" some time in the latter days.[31]

---

28. Doctrine and Covenants 109:64.
29. Deuteronomy 33:8–11.
30. Luke 1:5–6.
31. See Doctrine and Covenants 13.

Moses's Blessing on the Tribe of Joseph

Joseph's blessing from Moses is very like that received under Father Jacob's hand, but with some additional promises regarding the role of Ephraim and Manasseh:

> And of Joseph he said, Blessed of the Lord be his land, for the precious things of heaven, for the dew, and for the deep that coucheth beneath, And for the precious fruits brought forth by the sun, and for the precious things put forth by the moon, And for the chief things of the ancient mountains, and for the precious things of the lasting hills, And for the precious things of the earth and fullness thereof, and for the good will of him that dwelt in the bush [the burning bush]: let the blessing come upon the head of Joseph, and upon the top of the head of him that was separated from his brethren. His glory is like the firstling of his bullock, and his horns are like the horns of unicorns [Hebrew: the wild ox]: with them he shall push the people together to the ends of the earth: and they are the ten thousands of Ephraim, and they are the thousands of Manasseh.[32]

Ephraim and Manasseh have the responsibility of *pushing the people together*, or of gathering Israel. It is their sign of the ox that holds up the temple baptism fonts today: twelve oxen facing in all directions, with the charge to gather Israel and bring their brothers (and sisters) back to the Lord's covenant.

32. Deuteronomy 33:13–17.

CHAPTER 8

Judah and Joseph in the Land of Israel

Joshua (Ephraim) and Caleb (Judah) Lead the Way into the Promised Land

When it was at last time to enter within the promised land, it was again Joseph (Ephraim) and Judah who led the way in the persons of Joshua (Ephraim)[1] and Caleb (Judah).[2]

Moses had sent twelve men, one from each of the tribes, to "spy out" the land before the congregation of Israel entered it. Of those twelve, only two—Caleb and Joshua—showed the faith necessary to move forward in taking possession of the land under the direction and help of the Lord.[3] Hearing the other ten reports, the people were filled with fear and even went so far as to want to elect a captain to lead them back to Egypt.[4]

Joshua and Caleb stood up and urged, "Rebel not ye against the Lord, neither fear ye the people of the land . . . the Lord is with us: fear them not."[5]

---

1. Numbers 13:8.
2. Numbers 13:6.
3. See Numbers 13–14.
4. Numbers 14:1–4.
5. Numbers 14:9.

The people responded by wanting to stone Caleb and Joshua to death, but the Lord intervened in their behalf. He decreed that none of the people would be able to partake of the fruits of the land but would all die in the wilderness, while Joshua and Caleb would lead the next generation forward to at last inherit the promised "milk and honey" the land held for them.[6]

Again and again, the strength of leadership was evident in Judah, Joseph (Ephraim), and Levi (through Moses and Aaron). The story of the twelve spies illustrates how all were given equal opportunity to prove their faith, yet it was these three who rose to the test.

Rebellion over the Priesthood

This is not to say that the people readily followed their God-appointed leaders. In fact, one of the most dreadful plagues in Israelite history occurred because some of the men demanded the rights of the priesthood that were held by Aaron and his sons. One of their spokesmen accused Moses, "Ye take too much upon you, seeing all the congregation are holy, every one of them, and the Lord is among them: wherefore then lift ye up yourselves above the congregation of the Lord?"[7]

Although many of these rebels were from the tribe of Levi, who already had certain rights and duties for the tabernacle, they wanted more: they wanted to officiate in the higher priesthood duties within the tabernacle that pertained only to Aaron and his direct descendants. The Lord sent fire to consume those men and a pit to swallow them up. Surprisingly, the rest of the congregation responded with anger against Moses, Aaron, and the Lord. They had not been humbled by the terrible spectacle, but rather, their hearts were hardened in rebellion. The Lord then sent a plague, whereby thousands were killed.[8] Shortly afterward, the Lord instructed that a rod, or staff, from each tribe be placed within the tabernacle. He told the people that the rod of the man he chose would bud, thereby signifying the Lord's appointment to the priesthood. It was Aaron's rod that bloomed, and it

6. Numbers 14:30.
7. Numbers 16:3.
8. See Numbers 16.

was kept as a memorial for generations to remind the people that God would choose and appoint whom He would to His Holy Priesthood.[9]

Levites Have the Priesthood, and Therefore, No Land Inheritance

Because Aaron's family and the tribe of Levi received the gifts of the priesthood and the right to administer in the tabernacle temple, they did not receive a land inheritance. The Lord told them, "I am thy part and thine inheritance among the children of Israel."[10] They were to serve the tribes throughout the new land and to dwell within forty-eight cities allotted to them by the Lord.[11]

Joshua Appointed as the New Leader in Israel

Just before entering the promised land, the Lord instructed Moses to call and set apart Joshua as the new leader who would take his place.[12] Moses was going to finally rest and would not be going with the Israelites into their new inheritance in the land of Canaan.[13]

The Israelites to Drive Out the Canaanites from the Land

With today's viewpoint, it's rather painful to try to understand the Lord's instructions that the Israelites were to drive out the present inhabitants of the land of Canaan in order to receive their promise of inheriting that land. In the centuries that had passed since the Lord had promised Abraham that he and his posterity would own it, many others had moved in and made their homes there. However, the Lord was very clear in His commandment that

> Ye shall drive out all the inhabitants of the land from before you, and destroy all their pictures [stone figures], and destroy all their

9. See Numbers 17.
10. Numbers 18:20.
11. Numbers 35:7.
12. Numbers 27:18–23.
13. Deuteronomy 3:27; 32:48–52; Alma 45:19.

> molten images, and quite pluck down all their high places [hill shrines]. And ye shall dispossess the inhabitants of the land, and dwell therein: for I have given you the land to possess it.[14]

The Lord warned the Israelites that if they did not successfully drive out all of the inhabitants of the land then "It shall come to pass, that those which ye let remain of them shall be pricks in your eyes, and thorns in your sides, and shall vex you in the land wherein ye dwell."[15] This, indeed, came to pass, because the Israelites were ensnared by the idol worship of their neighbors, became apostate, entered into faulty alliances, and eventually were conquered and driven out of the land promised to Abraham.

Although Israel had rebelled continuously in their journey from Egypt, the Lord would keep his promise to Abraham to bring his posterity to Canaan again.[16] The Lord emphasized through his prophet, Moses, that the Israelites were not given the land due to any righteousness on their part, but rather because the people who were then dwelling in the land were ripe in their own wickedness.[17]

A Land Tied to Covenant and to God

The land they were about to enter was unique from all of its neighbors. The Lord referred to it as a "land flowing with milk and honey"[18] and told the Israelites that it was "a land of hills and valleys, and drinketh water of the rain of heaven: A land which the Lord thy God careth for: the eyes of the Lord thy God are always upon it, from the beginning of the year even unto the end of the year."[19]

This promised land was the envy of the surrounding nations, and all yearned to possess it, but God had designated it as His land and Israel as His people. The land was essentially tied to the covenant. This land, later to be called after its people, *Israel*, was to be a sanctuary, and, as such, was to be dedicated wholly to the Lord, with a temple

14. Numbers 33:52–53.
15. Numbers 33:55.
16. Genesis 15:13–14; 2 Nephi 29:14.
17. Deuteronomy 9:4–6.
18. Deuteronomy 11:9.
19. Deuteronomy 11:11–12.

in its midst. To emphasize this point, with every instruction regarding the taking of the land, there were also constant reminders of temple celebrations and offerings: the people were to remember to keep the Passover, the Feast of Tabernacles, and the Day of Atonement, as well as their daily offerings and sacrifices.[20] Their hearts were to be knit to God's in a relationship of covenant-chastity so deep and profound that God Himself referred to it as a marriage.[21]

Anciently, in order to help people better understand the serious nature of covenant making, the blessings for keeping covenants were explained, and the "curses" or consequences for breaking a covenant were also fully outlined.[22]

If the Israelites kept their covenants, the Lord promised to bless them, to make them fruitful in land and in posterity, and to make them "an holy nation" and "a kingdom of priests [and priestesses]."[23] But if the Israelites were to turn away from God and break their covenants, they would be vanquished and chastised at the hands of their enemies and lose their promised inheritance. Their understanding of the blessings of obedience and the consequences of disobedience was so vital that Moses instructed representatives from six of the tribes to stand on Mount Gerizim pronouncing the blessings of covenant keeping, while representatives of the remaining six tribes stood opposite on Mount Ebal declaring the curses of covenant breaking—all while the Israelites passed through the valley between them into the promised land.[24] As an added memorial, they were to build an altar for the Lord and write upon it all of the words of "this law" as soon as they passed over the Jordan River and into the new land. This was for a constant reminder that it was a covenant land dedicated by a covenant people to their Lord and God.[25]

---

20. See Numbers 4, 7, 9, 10, 15, 18–19, 28–29; Deuteronomy 4–6, 11–12, 16.
21. Jeremiah 3:14; Isaiah 54:5; see Lynda Cherry's *The Redemption of the Bride: God's Redeeming Love for His Covenant People.*
22. See Deuteronomy 28, 30.
23. Exodus 19:5–6; Deuteronomy 26:18–19.
24. Deuteronomy 27:11–13.
25. Deuteronomy 27:1–8.

Interestingly, Judah, Joseph, and Levi were among the tribes that were to pronounce the blessings of covenant.[26] Note that here, once again, Joseph is named as "one" that encompassed both Ephraim and Manasseh.

The Promised Land Divided among the Tribes

The tribes of Reuben, Gad, and half of Manasseh requested that their inheritance be outside of the land of Canaan, because they felt the land of Gilead and Jazer was good for grazing their cattle. This frustrated Moses, who feared that those tribes would separate themselves and not help fight the Canaanites with the rest of Israel. But the tribal leaders gave their word to assist their brethren in conquering the land, with the understanding that they would then return to dwell with their families east of the River Jordan.[27]

Through revelation, Moses was shown the boundaries of the promised land[28] and declared that Joshua (Ephraim) and Aaron's son, Eleazar the priest, would divide the land among the tribes.[29] This was no easy task, and the Lord encouraged Joshua with His first call to him: "Be strong and of a good courage: for unto this people shalt thou divide for an inheritance the land, which I sware unto their fathers to give them."[30]

Judah and Joseph Receive the First Tribal Land Allotments

Many battles later, the tribal allotments were confirmed. The first to receive an inheritance in the promised land was Caleb (Judah). Moses had promised Caleb his choice of land due to Caleb's integrity and faith when he and Joshua had stood apart in their assessment of the land more than forty years earlier. Caleb asked for, and was

---

26. Deuteronomy 27:12.
27. Numbers 32.
28. Deuteronomy 34:1–4.
29. Numbers 34:1–17.
30. Joshua 1:6.

granted, the sacred land of Hebron, where Abraham and Sarah were buried, together with the patriarchs Isaac and Jacob.[31]

After Caleb, the whole tribe of Judah received their land assignment, a choice allotment that included the sacred city that became Jerusalem, and Mount Moriah, where Abraham was willing to sacrifice his son, Isaac.[32]

The next tribe to receive an inheritance in the promised land was Joseph—named as just that, *Joseph,* in the scriptural account[33] but included Ephraim and half of the tribe of Manasseh. Joseph's assignment was Jericho, the sacred site of Beth-el, Luz, and Shechem, and another sacred site, Shiloh.[34] After they reminded Joshua that they were to receive a double portion due to the birthright, Ephraim and Manasseh received more, including Megiddo and the Jezreel Valley.[35] The two tribes were to share their inheritance as one under Joseph.

It is worth noting that the first place the tabernacle was set up was at Shiloh, within the inherited land belonging to Joseph, or Ephraim and Manasseh.[36]

Only after Judah and Joseph received their allotments were the remaining lands divided among the remaining tribes, which was done by lot, always with the reminder that Levi received no land inheritance, for "the Lord is their inheritance."[37]

For the reader's convenience, the chart of land inheritance is repeated on the following pages.

31. Joshua 14:6–15; Numbers 13:2–3, 6; 14:24; Genesis 23:17–20.
32. Joshua 15:1–63.
33. Joshua 16:1.
34. Joshua 16.
35. Joshua 17.
36. Joshua 18:1.
37. Joshua 18:4–7.

TWELVE SONS OF JACOB: NAMES, PATRIARCHAL BLESSINGS, and LAND INHERITANCES

Name/Meaning	Patriarchal Blessing	Land Allotment	Events
Reuben, "See, a Son" **Symbol: Man or Mandrake**	The beginning of Jacob's strength and excellency, but unstable and will not excel. Gen. 49:3–4	East of the Jordan River with Gad, and "East" Manasseh. Josh. 13:15–23	Lost birthright to sons of Joseph for defiling his father's bed. 1 Chron. 5:1; JST Gen. 48:5
	Let him live with many for posterity. Deut. 33:6		Convinced his brothers *not* to kill Joseph and later offered his sons as guarantee that he would bring Benjamin back safely to Joseph in Egypt. Gen. 37:21; 42:37
Simeon, "Hearing" **Symbol: Tower or City of Shechem**	An instrument of cruelty, will be divided and scattered in Israel. Gen. 49:5–7	Tribe of Simeon given a portion of the land of Judah. Josh. 19:1–9	Simeon and Levi slay a neighboring tribe. Gen. 34:25–31
		Tribe of Simeon given a portion of the land of Israel in Ezekiel's vision of the future. Ezek. 48:24	Tribe of Simeon joined with Judah and Joseph in conquering the Canaanites. Judg. 1

Name/Meaning	Patriarchal Blessing	Land Allotment	Events
			His descendants are known as mighty men of war. 1 Chron. 12:25
			Simeon's posterity in the celestial kingdom. Rev. 7:7
Levi, "Joined" **Symbol: Breastplate, Urim and Thummim**	An instrument of cruelty, will be divided and scattered in Israel. Gen. 49:5–7	No inheritance in the land save service in the temple; they receive a tithing from the people. Numb. 18:21, 23–24	Simeon and Levi slay a neighboring tribe. Gen. 34:25–31
	Let the Urim and Thummim be in their care; they have observed the word of the Lord and kept His covenant. Deut. 33:8–11		Levites to administer in the tabernacle and temple. Numb. 3:5–10; Levites "offered as an offering of the children of Israel," set apart by Aaron, given to the Lord in place of all firstborn sons. Numb. 8:7–16
			Levi blessed with priesthood, urim and thummim, and so forth. Deut. 33:8–11

Name/Meaning	Patriarchal Blessing	Land Allotment	Events
			Sons of Levi to offer an offering in righteousness in the latter days/ Millennium. D&C 13:1
			Levi's posterity in the celestial kingdom. Rev. 7:7
			Moses from Levi
Judah, "Praise" **Symbol: Lion**	His brethren will praise and bow down to him; like a lion; the scepter of Israel shall be his until the Messiah; prophecies of the Savior, who will come through his lineage. Gen. 49:8–12	Judah is given their portion in the southern kingdom, Jerusalem the capital. Josh. 15	King David from Judah; king first of Judah, then of all of Israel; the royal tribe. 2 Sam. 2:11
	The Lord will keep him strong and help him against enemies. Deut. 33:7		Only Judah left as a whole tribe after the destruction of Israel. 2 Kings 17:18
	Enmity between Ephraim, Manasseh, and Judah. Isa. 9:21		Judah's posterity in the celestial kingdom. Rev. 7:5

Name/Meaning	Patriarchal Blessing	Land Allotment	Events
Dan, "To Judge" **Symbol: Eagle with a Serpent in its Talons or Pair of Scales**	A judge of the people; a serpent and adder to those along the path. Gen. 49:16–18	Last tribe to receive a land allotment. They did not like the land given to them, so they attacked another city and took it over. Their new land was in northern boundary of Israel. Judg. 18	Held at bay by the Amorites; not able to drive them out of the land. Judg. 1:34
	A lion's whelp that shall leap from Bashan. Deut. 33:22		Set up false idols from the time they took their lands in Israel. Judg. 18:30–31
			Location of false idol set up by Jeroboam. 1 Kings 12:29
			The golden calves of Jeroboam remained in Dan. 2 Kings 10:29
Naphtali, "Wrestling" **Symbol: Hind; Deer**	A hind let loose; gives goodly words. Gen. 49:21	Land surrounding the Sea of Galilee. Josh. 19:32–39	Naphtali's posterity in the celestial kingdom. Rev. 7:6
	Satisfied with favor and full of the blessings of the Lord. Deut. 33:23		

Name/Meaning	Patriarchal Blessing	Land Allotment	Events
Gad, "A Troop" **Symbol: Troop of Horsemen**	A troop shall overcome him, but he shall overcome at last. Gen. 49:19	Did not want to cross Jordan; wanted to stay in the land of the Canaanites because of their cattle; allied with tribe of Reuben and "East" Manasseh. Numb. 32:1–5; Deut. 3:12–20	Mighty warriors; went after false gods; destroyed by Assyria. 1 Chron. 5:18–26
	He dwells as a lion tearing the arm with the crown of the head. He was a lawgiver, and gave the first portion to himself. Deut. 33:20–21		Gad's posterity in the celestial kingdom. Rev. 7:5
Asher, "My Happiness" **Symbol: Cup or Olive Tree**	His bread shall be fat and he shall eat royal dainties. Gen. 49:20	Shared inherited land with Manasseh; settled in the northwest, bordering on the Mediterranean and the Phoenician Empire; associated with seafaring. Joshua 17:7, 10–11; 19:24–31; Judg. 5	Heeded the call of King Hezekiah to come to Passover and renew covenants. 2 Chron. 30:11
	Blessed with children; dip feet in oil; shoes like iron and brass. Deut. 33:24–29 (Asher's land was rich with olive orchards. Wealthy.)		Asher's posterity in the celestial kingdom. Rev. 7:6

Name/Meaning	Patriarchal Blessing	Land Allotment	Events
Issachar, "A Reward" **Symbol: Ass or Sun, Moon, and Stars**	Compared to an ass between two burdens; saw that rest was good and the land pleasant and gave his shoulder to tribute; became a servant. Gen. 49:14–15	Primarily in the Jezreel Valley, between the tribes of Zebulun and Naphtali, the slopes of the eastern portion of lower Galilee. Josh. 19:17–23	Known for their wisdom; instrumental in the tribes uniting under King David; accepted the call of Hezekiah to come to Passover and renew covenants. 1 Chron. 12:32; 2 Chron. 30:18
	Issachar safe in his tents; shall offer sacrifices of righteousness, reap the treasures of the seas. Deut. 33:18–19		Issachar's posterity in the celestial kingdom. Rev. 7:7
Zebulun, "Dwelling" **Symbol: Ship**	Shall dwell at the haven of the sea with many ships. Gen. 49:13	Confused accounts about location. Patriarchal blessing says inheritance by the sea. Joshua 19:10–16 states Zebulun bordered on all sides by other tribes. No account of the sea or Galilee.	Lived amongst the Canaanites and became subject to forced labor. Judges 1:30
	Have abundance of the sea and treasures hid in the sand; offer righteous sacrifices. Deut. 33:18–19 (same as Issachar)		Heeded the call of King Hezekiah to come to Passover and renew covenants. 2 Chron. 30:11

Name/Meaning	Patriarchal Blessing	Land Allotment	Events
			Zebulun's posterity in the celestial kingdom. Rev. 7:8
Joseph, "Adding" **Symbol: Sheaf of Wheat**	Fruitful bough, branches run over the wall; made strong by the Lord although he was vexed and persecuted; blessed above (heaven) and below (earth); blessings of breast and womb; his blessings will prevail to the utmost hills.	Joseph's double-portion birthright was passed on to Ephraim (birthright) and Manasseh. See their inheritance below.	Joseph sold into Egypt by his brothers; he rose to power as a trusted advisor to Pharaoh and saved Israel during a famine.
	Blessed of the Lord be his land, for the precious things of heaven, for the dew, and for the deep . . . for precious fruits brought forth by the sun and the precious things put forth by the moon; for the chief things of the ancient mountains, and for the precious things of the everlasting hills, and for the precious things of the earth and fulness thereof. Deut. 33:13–16		

Name/Meaning	Patriarchal Blessing	Land Allotment	Events
	Joseph prevailed and obtained the birthright through obedience and righteousness; he shall be a light to Israel and deliver Israel from captivity and bondage and bring salvation unto them. JST Gen. 48:5–11		
	A promise that a fruitful branch shall come from Joseph; a prophet from Joseph's loins (not the Messiah) shall rise up to deliver the people from bondage; a branch shall be carried to a far country and will be remembered in the covenants of the Lord; in the latter days they shall bring forth light and help deliver Israel from captivity; a seer from Joseph's loins shall be raised up who shall be called Joseph; he will bring people back to a knowledge of the covenants and do a great work; he will bring the word of Joseph's seed to all the world and join with the word of Judah to confound false doctrine. JST Gen. 50:24–26; 2 Nephi 3:4–22		

Name/Meaning	Patriarchal Blessing	Land Allotment	Events
Benjamin "Son of My Right Hand" **Symbol: Wolf**	Like a ravening wolf in the morning, will divide the spoil in the evening. Gen. 49:27	Land given between Ephraim to the north and Judah to the south, prime location; Bethel, Jerusalem, Jericho—three holy cities given to Benjamin to share with Judah. Josh. 18:11–28	The brothers tested by Joseph as to whether they will protect Benjamin in Egypt; Judah steps forward to offer himself a ransom for Benjamin. Gen. 44:18–34
	Benjamin to dwell between the shoulders of the Lord (Joseph and Judah); beloved of the Lord; will dwell safely. Deut. 33:12		The tribe of Benjamin known to be mighty warriors. 1 Chron. 12:2 Benjamin aligned with Judah. 1 Kings 12:21
			Tribe of Benjamin almost annihilated by the other tribes over the assault on the Levite's concubine. Judg. 19–21
			King Saul from Benjamin

Name/Meaning	Patriarchal Blessing	Land Allotment	Events
Ephraim, "Fruitful" **Sign: Ox**	Birthright son of Joseph; shall become a multitude of nations. Gen. 48:17–20; 1 Chron. 5:1–2	Jordan at Jericho to the waters of Jericho on the east into the wilderness, through the hill country to Bethel, Bethel to Luz, ending at the sea; the holy cities of Shechem and Shiloh were within Ephraim's boundaries; shared with the "western" half of Manasseh. Josh. 16; 17:17	Front (or rear) lines of Israel's safety and defense; brought up the rearward of the camp of Israel; in the front lines in fighting the Canaanites under Joshua (an Ephraimite).
	A future great seer will come through his lineage. JST Gen. 50:24–38		Joshua from Ephraim. Num. 13:8 Samuel the prophet, an Ephraimite. 1 Sam. 1:1
	With horns like a unicorn (or a wild ox) Ephraim will push together the ten thousands of people of the earth (to gather Israel). Deut. 33:13–17		King Jeroboam of Ephraim divided Israel and led them into apostasy. 1 Kings 12:19–20, 25–31; 14:7–12
	The Lord will redeem Ephraim, His "firstborn." Jer. 31:9		Joseph Smith from Ephraim. *Journal of Discourses* 2:268–69
	Ephraim will greet and crown the incoming lost tribes. D&C 133:26–34		

Name/Meaning	Patriarchal Blessing	Land Allotment	Events
	Those who are rebellious will not be counted as "the blood of Ephraim." D&C 64:36		
Manasseh, "Making to Forget" **Sign: Unicorn or Ox**	He will be great but fewer in number than Ephraim. Gen. 48:17–20	Land on both sides of the Jordan (as half-tribe inheritances); included the land of Gilead, some of the richest soil in Israel. Joshua 13:29–31 The land on the western side was shared with Ephraim. Josh. 17:17 (The western side included Mounts Ebal, Gerizim, Gilboa, and Carmel.)	Responded to Hezekiah's invitation to Passover and a healing of Israel after their destruction by Assyria. 2 Chron. 30:11
	Manasseh, with Ephraim, will help gather Israel. Deut. 33:13–17		Gideon from Manasseh. Judges 6:15
			Lehi from Manasseh. Alma 10:3

Marriage Outside of the Covenant Leads to Apostasy, War, and Enslavement

Shortly after having taken possession of the land, and after Joshua's death, the Israelites fell prey to all that the Lord and His prophets had warned them against: going after the gods of the Canaanites who had possessed the land and dwelt amongst them.[38]

The Israelites intermarried with the Canaanites, Hittites, Amorites, Perizzites, Hivites and Jebusites, out of the covenant, and their children were raised without knowing the Lord Jehovah, or what it meant to be covenant Israel.[39] Their new alliances turned against the Israelites, constantly overcoming them in battle, and enslaving them. The Lord raised up "judges" (not prophets) such as Deborah, Gideon and Samson to lead the Israelites in battle, but there was a never-ending cycle of betrayal and violence among the tribes and their neighbors.

---

38. Judges 2:10–23.
39. Judges 3:4–7.

CHAPTER 9

Israel United under Judah (King David)

David Defends the Name of the Lord

INTO THAT NEVER-ENDING CYCLE OF WAR AND VIOLENCE CAME THE shepherd-warrior David. He was just a boy when he was anointed king by the prophet Samuel.[1] He was still a youth too small to wear a man's armor when he confronted the giant Goliath. David did not go against Goliath in a spirit of boastful bravado, but rather to defend the name and reputation of Israel's God, whom Goliath and the Philistines were mocking. David told Goliath:

> Thou comest to me with a sword, and with a spear, and with a shield: but I come to thee in the name of the Lord of hosts, the God of the armies of Israel, whom thou hast defied. This day will the Lord deliver thee into mine hand; and I will smite thee . . . that all the earth may know that there is a God in Israel.[2]

1. 1 Samuel 16:13.
2. 1 Samuel 17:45–46.

David Waits upon the Lord

Even after defeating the giant, David was circumspect. He did not reveal that he had already been anointed by the prophet Samuel to be the next king of Israel. The chronicler expresses repeatedly that "David behaved himself wisely in all his ways."[3] Although the people loved David and feared Saul's moods, David did not seek to usurp Saul's throne, but rather declared that he would not lift his hand against the Lord's anointed.[4] He played the harp and sang for Saul and repeatedly sought peace with him, even when Saul tried to kill him.[5]

God had told Samuel, "Man looketh on the outward appearance, but the Lord looketh on the heart."[6] David's heart was set on the Lord. He constantly asked the Lord what he should do. "Shall I go and smite these Philistines?"[7] "Will the men of this city deliver me into Saul's hands?"[8] And, after Saul's death, when all the people were holding their breath to see what David would do, David still asked God: "Shall I go up into any of the cities of Judah?"[9] That trip into the land of Judah and his heritage was inevitable and brought to pass Samuel's prophecy of David's mission: the tribe of Judah came together and anointed David to be king "over the house of Judah."[10]

Abner, the captain of Saul's army, did not follow after David but set up Ishbosheth, Saul's son, as king over the other tribes of Israel.[11] David never raised a hand against Saul or his descendants, but rather sought to protect them. He did not fight for the right to rule or take it by force, even though Samuel had anointed him to become Israel's king so many years earlier. He waited, trusting in the Lord's timing.

---

3. 1 Samuel 18:5, 14.
4. 1 Samuel 24:6, 10; 26:9, 11, 23.
5. 1 Samuel 19:10; 20:31.
6. 1 Samuel 16:7.
7. 1 Samuel 23:2.
8. 1 Samuel 23:12.
9. 2 Samuel 2:1.
10. 2 Samuel 2:4.
11. 2 Samuel 2:8–9.

David had been king over Judah for seven and a half years when, upon Ishbosheth's death, all the tribes of Israel came to David and anointed him as king over all Israel.[12]

The formerly warring tribes came to David and declared, "Behold, we are thy bone and thy flesh . . . and the Lord said to thee, Thou shalt feed my people Israel, and thou shalt be a captain over Israel."[13] Their words were familial and intimate, almost like a marriage proposal. Alfred Edersheim wrote, "Such enthusiasm had never before been witnessed! Not bidden, but voluntarily they came."[14] And "David perceived that the Lord had established him for his people Israel's sake."[15]

David came to the throne with the desire for a united Israel under God. Under David's rule, not only were the tribes united for the first time, but they finally filled the boundaries promised to Abraham and were at last viewed as a nation by those who surrounded them.

A Kingdom of Israel Centered upon God, with the Temple at Its Heart

David was only thirty years old when he became the king of all Israel, the same age that Jesus was when He began His ministry and was proclaimed as the Messiah, the Son of David. He ruled over united Israel for thirty-three years.

David made his capital city Jerusalem,[16] and eager to dedicate it to the Lord, he brought the tabernacle and the ark of the Lord into the city so that his kingdom would clearly be centered upon God.

Dressed in the linen ephod of a priest, David danced before the Lord and sang with joy and thanksgiving.[17] Officiating in the role of priest, David offered the sacrifices before the Lord and blessed the people in the name of the Lord.[18] David officiated as both a king and a priest in Israel, personifying the promise inherent in the covenant

---

12. 2 Samuel 5:1–3.
13. 2 Samuel 5:1–2.
14. Alfred Edersheim, *Bible History, Old Testament*, 520.
15. 2 Samuel 5:12.
16. 2 Samuel 5:6–7.
17. 2 Samuel 6:14–15; 1 Chronicles 15:27–29.
18. 2 Samuel 6:17–18; 24:25; 1 Chronicles 16:2.

invitation of becoming "an holy nation, a kingdom of priests."[19] Although little is known of the intervening years, David followed the pattern of Melchizedek, who had once reigned as king and priest in the holy city of Salem,[20] now David's Jerusalem.

David's great desire was to give honor to the Lord and build a temple to house the tabernacle and its furnishings.[21] David mourned over the fact that he, as king, had a palace, but the Lord dwelt only in a tent.

The Messiah to be Born of David's Posterity

As the Lord had promised, He looked upon the heart,[22] and seeing David's heart of love and dedication, He responded to David by promising him that He, God, would build *David* a "house." The Lord told David: "And thine house and thy kingdom shall be established forever before thee: thy throne shall be established forever,"[23] thus confirming the earlier promise to Judah that the Messiah, the King of kings and Lord of lords, would not only come from the tribe of Judah, but also from the House of David.[24]

David's reaction to the Lord's promise says so much about him:

> Who am I, O Lord God? And what is my house, that thou hast brought me hitherto? . . . And what one nation in the earth is like thy people, even like Israel, whom God went to redeem for a people to himself, and to make him a name . . . For thou hast confirmed to thyself thy people Israel to be a people unto thee forever: and thou, Lord, art become their God.[25]

In many ways, David foreshadowed the life and mission of the Savior, Jesus Christ.

---

19. Exodus 19:5–6.
20. See Genesis 14:18.
21. 2 Samuel 7:1–3.
22. 1 Samuel 16:7.
23. 2 Samuel 7:16; 1 Chronicles 17:10–14.
24. See Genesis 49:8–12.
25. 2 Samuel 7:18, 23–24; 1 Chronicles 17:16–27.

King David	Jesus Christ
Name means "Beloved"	Jesus is the "Beloved Son"
Birthplace: Bethlehem	Birthplace: Bethlehem
Shepherd/King of Israel	Shepherd/King of Israel
United Israel for the First Time	Will Unite Israel Forever
Established Jerusalem as the Spiritual and Political Center of Israel	Will Establish Jerusalem as the Spiritual Center with Zion as the Political Center of the Millennium
Mighty Warrior	Will be seen as the Mighty Warrior at the Second Coming (Revelation 19:11–16)
Loyal, Devoted Friend (Jonathan and others)	"Greater Love Hath No Man Than This: That a Man Lay Down His Life for His Friends" (John 15:13)
Saw Himself as a Servant/King/Priest	The Servant/King/Priest
Gave all Glory to God	Gave all Glory to God

David Is Shown a Vision of the Temple

Although the Lord did not permit David to build the temple,[26] He nevertheless showed David in vision the pattern after which the temple was to be built. "All this," David claimed, "the Lord made me understand in writing by his hand upon me, even all the works of this pattern."[27]

For David, the temple was a living thing. It was ever on his mind as he worked through all the details of its furnishings and construction.[28] When he passed on the duty of building the temple to his son, Solomon, David had already collected all of the materials necessary

26. 1 Chronicles 28:3.
27. 1 Chronicles 28:12–19.
28. 1 Chronicles 28:11–19.

for its completion.[29] He counseled his son that "the house that is to be builded for the Lord must be exceeding magnifical" and told him that building it would be the most important work of his reign.[30]

More, David composed much of the temple liturgy and worship under the direction of the Spirit. Although we cannot attribute all of the Psalms to David (or even most of them), many of those known to be his are rich in prophecy and were used in temple celebrations.[31] The chronicler records that at the time of David's dance with the entry of the ark, he wrote that his people should "worship the Lord in the beauty of holiness" . . . for "his mercy endureth forever" . . . and "we are a covenant people."[32]

David set the Levites in the order that had been ordained at Sinai and commanded them to cleanse and sanctify themselves. At the time of his death, there were 38,000 Levites, 4,000 of whom were assigned to sing songs of praise.[33] According to historian Alfred Edersheim, this was the first time the service of praise was introduced in the public worship of Israel.[34]

David's love for God and the temple was contagious: he ably transmitted his love to his people, who themselves became caught up in a heartfelt desire to build the temple and offer up all they had in that endeavor.[35] What a change David had wrought in the previously warring tribes, now united with one focus and goal: to fully become the people of God, even a covenant people.[36] David sang:

> *O ye seed of Israel his servant, ye children of Jacob, his chosen ones.*
> *He is the Lord our God; his judgments are in all the earth.*
> *Be ye mindful always of his covenant;*
> *the word which he commanded to a thousand generations;*

---

29. 1 Chronicles 22; 28:14–18; 29:2–5.
30. 1 Chronicles 22:5.
31. See Jeffrey M. Bradshaw's "What Was the Religious Role of Music in the Life and Times of David?"; Psalm 118; 1 Chronicles 16:4–36.
32. See 1 Chronicles 16:8–36, 41.
33. 1 Chronicles 15:12–15; 23:3–5.
34. Alfred Edersheim, *Bible History, Old Testament*, 526.
35. 1 Chronicles 29:9.
36. 1 Chronicles 29:20.

Even of the covenant which he made with Abraham,
and of his oath unto Isaac;
And hath confirmed the same to Jacob for a law,
and to Israel for an everlasting covenant . . .
Sing unto the Lord, all the earth;
shew forth from day to day his salvation.
. . . give unto the Lord the glory due unto his name;
bring an offering, and come before him:
worship the Lord in the beauty of holiness.[37]

37. 1 Chronicles 16:13–29.

CHAPTER 10

Judah and Joseph Divided

THE UNIFICATION AND PEACE BETWEEN THE TRIBES WAS SHORT LIVED.

Political Marriages and False Idols

Solomon, David's son, was at first humble and compliant before the Lord. All he desired was wisdom to know how to govern his people and lead them in righteousness.[1] He built and dedicated the first temple in Jerusalem, officiating as a priest and king before his people.[2] However, he entered into political marriages with women from neighboring kingdoms, and in a spirit of religious tolerance, allowed them to bring their gods with them into Israel, a land that had been dedicated entirely to the Lord Jehovah, the God of Abraham, Isaac, and Jacob. Solomon built groves and places of worship for the idols, and his people followed his example, quickly giving in to idolatrous practices, while at the same time, professing obedience to Jehovah at the temple in Jerusalem.[3]

1. 1 Kings 3:7–12.
2. See 1 Kings 8; 2 Chronicles 6–7.
3. 1 Kings 11:1–10.

"And the Lord was angry with Solomon, because his heart was turned from the Lord God of Israel, which had appeared unto him twice."[4] As a result, the Lord told Solomon that the kingdom would be divided. His family would no longer reign over a united Israel. Because of the promise the Lord had made to David, Judah would always have a man on the throne in Jerusalem, but he would reign over Judah alone.[5] The other tribes would not follow.[6]

Jeroboam of Ephraim and Rehoboam of Judah Divide the Kingdom

The Ephraimite who fulfilled the prophecy of dividing the kingdom, Jeroboam, brought grief upon his people by taking them immediately into apostasy. Jeroboam is first introduced in the Bible when Solomon made him a ruler over the house of Joseph.[7] As had occurred with David when he was yet a youth, a prophet foretold Jeroboam's future as king of the ten tribes of Israel but warned him that he must walk in the covenant of the Lord in order to receive the blessings of that covenant for his family and his people.[8] The prophet also confirmed that David's posterity was to reign in Jerusalem as the Lord had promised. Much as Saul had done before him, Solomon sought to kill Jeroboam in a fit of jealousy when he heard of the prophecy. Jeroboam fled to Egypt until after Solomon's death, but he returned when the Israelites were debating on whether to follow Solomon's son, Rehoboam, as king.[9]

In all fairness, despite the prophecy concerning him, Jeroboam did not wrest the kingdom from Rehoboam until he and the other tribal leaders had questioned Rehoboam about his goals as king, specifically about the level of taxation he would implement over his people. When Rehoboam "answered the people roughly" on this issue, promising to impose heavier taxes than they had yet known, the Israelites

4. 1 Kings 11:9.
5. 1 Kings 12:20.
6. 1 Kings 11:11–13.
7. 1 Kings 11:28.
8. 1 Kings 11:31–38.
9. 1 Kings 11:40; 12:1–17.

rebelled against him. All but the tribes of Judah and Benjamin turned to Jeroboam and asked him to become the "king over all Israel."[10]

Ephraim Leads the Kingdom in the North into Apostasy

Thus occurred the separation of the ten tribes—called *Israel*—from Judah and Benjamin in the south. Ever after, those in the north would be called by various titles, including the *Northern Kingdom*, *Israel*, *Ephraim* (as the leading tribe of Joseph), and *Samaria*, the capital city. The use of these names often causes confusion as to whom, exactly, is being spoken of. Going forward, historically and geographically, the name *Israel* was seldom used to represent the entire covenant nation. Only in prophecies of a future day of gathering and restoration does the name *Israel* represent the name of God's covenant family.

Jeroboam completely disregarded the cautionary instruction he had received that he must lead his people in the ways of the Lord. As soon as he set up his own kingdom, he installed two golden calves at the northern and southern borders of his new realm. Jeroboam feared that if his people made the obligatory trek to the temple in Jerusalem for the designated feast days, they would turn against him and reunite with Judah. He told his people that it was "too much" for them to make the long journey to the temple and that they could worship the calves at Bethel and Dan instead. He appointed priests who were not Levites to officiate at the shrines and established alternate feast days for celebrations.[11] Despite immediate warnings through the Lord's prophets, Jeroboam would not repent of his idolatry and earned the appellation in the scriptures of "*Jeroboam, who made Israel to sin*."[12]

The scriptural record characterizes every ruler of the northern tribes as evil or wicked. Twenty kings ruled in Israel until destruction

---

10. 1 Kings 11:12–20; 2 Chronicles 10:13–19.
11. 1 Kings 12:25–33; 2 Chronicles 11:14–16; 15:9–10. Note that at this time many of the Levites left their assignments in the north and went to live in the southern kingdom of Judah where they could faithfully serve before the Lord in the temple. In addition, faithful covenant keepers from all of the tribes left the north to live in the south near the temple.
12. 1 Kings 14:16; 2 Kings 10:29; 13:1–2, 11.

by the Assyrians: five different family dynasties, all short lived, ending by assassination or violence. Seven monarchs were murdered, and one committed suicide. The prophets Elijah, Elisha, Amos, and Hosea ministered in the Northern Kingdom, calling on the kings and people to repent and to return to Jehovah. Isaiah and Micah, prophets of Judah, also warned the people of the Northern Kingdom of the coming destruction if they did not repent.

In Israel, the Northern Kingdom, apostasy prevailed. Despite the efforts of the prophets, the kings in the north never returned fully to the worship of Jehovah as Lord.

We can only wonder why the people were so susceptible in following the foolish whims of their leaders. How could they so easily reject the Lord after they had witnessed so many miracles in their nation's life? How much of Israel's disintegration was due to tribal rivalry, and how much to ignorance of God's word and covenant? How likely are we to fall prey to the same blindness?

Cycles of Apostasy in the Southern Kingdom of Judah

Meanwhile, Solomon's son, Rehoboam, was also leading his people into apostasy. As the son of one of Solomon's foreign wives,[13] we can only suppose that he had been introduced to the gods of his mother, and therefore allowed idols and groves to be built throughout Judah, where all sorts of abominations occurred, including fertility rites as part of worship.[14] How quickly the covenant people departed from their God!

The apostasy in the south led to the spoliation of the temple in Jerusalem. James E. Talmage wrote:

> The glorious pre-eminence of this splendid structure was of brief duration. Thirty-four years after its dedication, and but five years subsequent to the death of Solomon, its decline began; and this decline was soon to develop into general spoliation, and finally to become an actual desecration. Solomon the king, the man of wisdom, the master-builder, had been led astray by the wiles of idolatrous

13. 1 Kings 14:21.
14. 1 Kings 14:21–24.

> women, and his wayward ways had fostered iniquity in Israel. *The nation was no longer a unit;* there were factions and sects, parties and creeds, some worshipping on the hilltops, others under green trees, each party claiming excellence for its own particular shrine. The Temple soon lost its sanctity. The gift became depreciated by the perfidy [betrayal] of the giver, and Jehovah withdrew His protecting presence from the place no longer holy.[15]

The prophecy that the Davidic line would reign and control the house of Judah was fulfilled. Twenty rulers reigned over Judah from the death of Solomon to the fall of Jerusalem and the Jews' captivity and exile at the hands of the Babylonians. Twelve are characterized as evil or wicked. Four advanced their nation economically and religiously. Prophets called to minister to Judah were Micaiah, Isaiah, Micah, Nahum, Habakkuk, Zephaniah, Lehi, Jeremiah, and Ezekiel. As we study the scriptural accounts, we see the conditions of Judah swing according to the faithfulness of king and people. There were times of great righteousness as well as wickedness.

The scriptures record that many members of other tribes migrated over the years to the Southern Kingdom and became a part of the nation of Judah.[16] This perhaps helps us understand how Lehi (of Manasseh) came to be in Jerusalem.[17] However, it does add to confusion about who "the Jews" are—whether they are the people of one tribe, or a conglomeration of peoples from various tribes who came to live in the south. For the purposes of this book, we will try to distinguish the people of Judah as an individual tribe so that we can follow their history and tribal responsibilities.

False Gods and Idols

Baal—The sun god, the supreme god of the Phoenicians; a fertility god. Those who worshiped Baal felt that such worship would ensure the generative and reproductive power of the soil and their animals as well as themselves. In such worship, with its emphasis on fertility,

15. James E. Talmage, *House of the Lord: A Study of Holy Sanctuaries Ancient and Modern*, 6–7; emphasis added.
16. 2 Chronicles 15:9.
17. 1 Nephi 5:16; Alma 10:3.

such practices as ritual prostitution of both sexes became rampant. Those who engaged in such practices were referred to by the Lord as *sodomites.* Other terms such as *high places, images* (idols), *groves, high hills,* and *green trees* were all associated with the false and reprehensible forms of worship.[18]

Ashtoreth/Asherah—Female companion to Baal, or "God's wife," with 450 priests/priestesses. Pagan fertility goddess, she was notorious for the prostitution cults associated with her temples.

Milcom/Molech/Moloch—Molech's worshipers dug a large, deep pit, filled it with wood, ignited the fire, and then sacrificed humans there. "The abomination of the children of Ammon, a fire god, worshiped by passing children through or burning them in fire."[19] Sometimes an image of Molech was made out of metal, the arms hollow. Fire would be built in the arms, and a child placed upon them.

Chemosh—"The destroyer, subduer, or fish god." This was the God of the Moabites and the Ammonites, which they frequently offered human sacrifice to thinking it would appease his anger. The sacrifice of children as a burnt offering is a central part of both Chemosh and Molech/Moloch worship.

Dissension and War between the Tribes

The author of the book of Kings tells us that "there was war between Rehoboam and Jeroboam all their days."[20] And so the tribes fought, led by Judah and Joseph, each seeking to destroy and annex the other. King Asa of Judah entered into a treaty with Syria to go against King Baasha of Israel.[21] Years later, King Jehoash of Israel went against King Amaziah of Judah and broke down the wall of Jerusalem, taking the vessels from the temple back to his capital city of Samaria.[22] Yet again, King Pekah of Israel captured a multitude of Jewish prisoners and

---

18. "Idolatry: Ancient and Modern," *Old Testament Student Manual.*
19. Bible Dictionary, "Baal," 733.
20. 1 Kings 14:30.
21. 2 Chronicles 16:1–4.
22. 2 Kings 14:11–14; 2 Chronicles 25:21–24.

took them to Samaria.[23] Despite the warnings of the prophet Isaiah, King Ahaz of Judah reached out to the king of Assyria for help and triggered the eventual Assyrian conquest of northern Israel and the captivity of the ten tribes.[24]

---

23. 2 Chronicles 28:8.
24. 2 Chronicles 28:16.

CHAPTER 11

Joseph (Ephraim) and the Ten Tribes Conquered and Scattered

The Assyrian Conquest of the Ten Tribes—Ephraim Is Scattered

The promised destruction of northern Israel (the ten tribes) had come: the kings and people failed to listen to the warning voices of the prophets and persisted in depravity and wickedness. In 738 BC, the Northern Kingdom of Israel was attacked for the first time by the superpower that would eventually annihilate them: Assyria.[1] Israel allied themselves and joined forces with their old enemy, Syria, but all fell before the ferocity of the Assyrian army. This attack would be the first of many.

Israel became a tributary to Assyria, paying hefty taxes that bankrupted a nation that had been spoiled by wars and famine for many years. In 735 BC, the kings of Israel and Syria formed another alliance in an effort to throw off the Assyrian stronghold over their countries. They were soundly defeated, and the first transportation of the

1. 2 Kings 15:19.

population occurred, with many inhabitants of the northern boundaries of the nation being carried away.[2]

Instead of turning to the Lord for help, the new kings of Israel and Syria again formed a coalition in 734 BC and went against *Judah*, taking many prisoners and some land.[3] Isaiah was the prophet in Judah. He warned the king, Ahaz, not to form an alliance with Assyria for help in defending himself against Israel and Syria.[4] Isaiah also prophesied that both Israel and Syria would be destroyed by the Assyrians.[5]

Judean King Ahaz failed to follow Isaiah's instructions and sent tribute money to the Assyrian king, who did not give him the needed help.[6] In his desperation, Ahaz offered his son as a sacrifice to Moloch and incorporated Assyrian altars and worship in the temple at Jerusalem.[7]

In 732 BC, Assyria set up a vassal king in northern Israel, Hoshea, but even this king rebelled against the Assyrians in 726 BC and refused to pay tribute.[8] Again, the brutal Assyrian army encamped about Israel, and a siege began that lasted three years.[9] By the end of it in 722–721 BC, almost the entire nation of Israel was carried away captive to foreign lands, becoming the ten lost tribes.[10] In their place, the Assyrians resettled the conquered and depopulated territory of Israel with people from Mesopotamia.[11] Those new citizens superstitiously desired to know how to worship "the god of the land" of Israel, and "priests" were sent to instruct them. They added Jehovah to their already full pantheon and worshipped a variety of deity.[12] The author of 2 Kings states, "So these nations feared the Lord, and served their graven images, both their children, and their children's children: as

2. 2 Kings 15:29.
3. 2 Kings 15:36–37; 2 Chronicles 27:6–8.
4. Isaiah 7:1–6.
5. Isaiah 7:17–25; 8:1–8; 9:8–12.
6. 2 Kings 16:8–9; 2 Chronicles 28:20–21.
7. 2 Kings 16:3, 10–18.
8. 2 Kings 17:3–4.
9. 2 Kings 17:5; 18:10.
10. 2 Kings 17:6–24.
11. 2 Kings 17:24–34.
12. 2 Kings 17:27–33.

did their fathers, so do they unto this day."[13] (Note: dates are approximate and vary even in the *Old Testament Student Manual.*)

This abbreviated history helps to partially explain the reason for the hatred of the Jews toward the "Samaritans"— the people they considered half-breed spoilers of the true religion. That hatred only escalated after the return of the Jews from their own captivity in Babylon, when after their refusal of help from the Samaritans in rebuilding the temple, the Samaritans sought to deter the rebuilding of Jerusalem and its walls.[14]

What of the Promises to Joseph?

The house of Joseph, led by Ephraim, was lost and gone from the promised lands. They had led the other tribes into apostasy and betrayed the Lord and their brethren by doing so.

What was to become of Joseph's promise of abundance and prosperity? What was to become of Joseph's stewardship and promise of leadership in Israel? Were the promises and covenants of God to be thwarted by individual wickedness? We shall see that despite the failings of men, God's promises are sure, and those given to both Joseph and Judah are still in the process of being fulfilled.

13. 2 Kings 17:41.
14. See Nehemiah, chapters 4 and 9.

CHAPTER 12

Judah Conquered and Taken into Captivity

THERE WERE PERIODS OF LIGHT IN THE SOUTHERN KINGDOM OF Judah when kings such as Jehoshaphat,[1] Hezekiah,[2] and Josiah[3] came to the throne and did away with the idols and groves and renewed the covenant with the Lord, but those periods were short lived.

King Hezekiah's Religious Revival

Between the first and final deportations of the people of the Northern Kingdom, in 728 BC, Hezekiah came to the throne of Judah.[4] With his accession to the throne came a great religious revival. The prophet Isaiah, who had withdrawn from court during the reign of Hezekiah's wicked father, Ahaz, became Hezekiah's trusted counselor and guide.

Hezekiah began immediately to remove the Canaanite and Assyrian shrines his father had placed throughout Judah.

1. 2 Chronicles 17:1–6.
2. See 2 Kings 18–19; 2 Chronicles 29.
3. See 2 Kings 22–23.
4. 2 Kings 18:1–10.

> He removed the high places, and brake the images, and cut down the groves, and brake in pieces the brazen serpent that Moses had made: for unto those days the children of Israel did burn incense to it . . . He trusted in the Lord God of Israel; so that after him was none like him among all the kings of Judah, nor any that were before him.[5]
>
> In the first year of his reign, in the first month [he] opened the doors of the house of the Lord, and repaired them.[6]

He ordered the Levites to cleanse themselves and then to cleanse the temple. "Now it is in mine heart to make a covenant with the Lord God of Israel, that his fierce wrath may turn away from us," he said.[7] The temple was cleansed and sanctified within eight days, and "Hezekiah the king rose early, and gathered the rulers of the city, and went up to the house of the Lord."[8]

Hezekiah humbly asked that the high priest and the Levites return to their duties as outlined by the Lord in the scriptures and to offer sacrifices in righteousness and with exactness.[9] "And when they had made an end of offering, the king and all that were present with him bowed themselves, and worshipped."[10]

Like David before him, Hezekiah's humble submission and desire to follow God with a pure heart greatly blessed his people.

Hezekiah Seeks Reconciliation with Those Left in the North

Hezekiah also sought for the unity and welfare of those who were left of his brothers and sisters of Israel. When the atonement offering was made at the temple, Hezekiah commanded that the offering should be made for *all* of Israel, not just those who were in Jerusalem or of Judah and Benjamin.[11] He then sent letters to all Israel and

5. 2 Kings 18:4–5.
6. 2 Chronicles 29:3.
7. 2 Chronicles 29:10.
8. 2 Chronicles 29:20.
9. 2 Chronicles 29:25–28.
10. 2 Chronicles 29:29.
11. 2 Chronicles 29:24.

Judah, inviting them to "*come to the house of the Lord* at Jerusalem, to keep the Passover unto the Lord God of Israel."[12]

Hezekiah's letter to those who yet remained in the Northern Kingdom reveals his understanding about the need for a united Israel centered on God. He wrote:

> Ye children of Israel, turn again unto the Lord God of Abraham, Isaac, and Israel, and he will return to the remnant of you that are escaped out of the hand of the kings of Assyria. Now be ye not stiffnecked, as your fathers were, but yield yourselves unto the Lord, and enter into his sanctuary, which he hath sanctified for ever: and serve the Lord your God, that the fierceness of his wrath may turn away from you. For if ye turn again unto the Lord, your brethren and your children shall find compassion before them that lead them captive, so that they shall come again into this land: for the Lord your God is gracious and merciful, and will not turn away his face from you, if ye return unto him.[13]

Most of the remnant in the Northern Kingdom "laughed [the messengers] to scorn and mocked them."[14] But some did "humble themselves" and came to Jerusalem.

Hezekiah's leadership in turning the people's hearts to God, to His temple, and to His covenant had brought about a community built on the principles of Zion, because they then turned their hearts to caring for one another, even to those who had been lost or whom they considered corrupt (those of the Northern Kingdom). They sought to share the blessings of the covenant with all.

A Miraculous Passover

The words of the chronicler are poignant in describing this miraculous Passover: even though those who came from the Northern Kingdom had not "cleansed themselves" and were therefore not qualified to partake of the Passover according to the Law, Hezekiah prayed

---

12. 2 Chronicles 30:1–5; emphasis added.
13. 2 Chronicles 30:6–9.
14. 2 Chronicles 30:10.

in their behalf asking the Lord to pardon them. "And the Lord hearkened to Hezekiah and healed the people."[15]

During the seven days of the feast, Hezekiah had the Levites teach all the people the Law (or covenant), and they all rejoiced in it. By the end of that required seven days, the people decided to keep seven additional days "with gladness."[16] "So there was great joy in Jerusalem: for since the time of Solomon . . . there was not the like in Jerusalem."[17]

Following this unique Passover celebration, the people were so heartened that they took it upon themselves to tear down the idols and images throughout the land, performing this act of their own free will, and declaring themselves as fully committed to the God of Israel and His Law and covenant.[18]

As proof of their commitment to their covenants, the people worked, sowed, and gleaned until they had brought forth an abundance of crops and flocks such as had not been seen previously. They brought the abundance into the courts of the temple as a tithe so that all people might have enough and to spare.[19]

The chronicler writes of Hezekiah: "And in every work that he began in the service of the house of God, and in the Law, and in the commandments to seek his God, he did it with all his heart, and prospered."[20]

Hezekiah and Jerusalem Escape Destruction

In his reliance upon the Lord, Hezekiah broke the old alliance his father had made with Assyria and refused to pay tribute. As a result, in 714 BC, the Assyrian king, Sennacherib, invaded Judah and captured many of its fortified cities.[21] A great host encamped against Jerusalem. One of the commanding officers, Rab-shakeh, threatened and taunted the leaders of Jerusalem:

---

15. 2 Chronicles 30:18–20.
16. 2 Chronicles 30:21–23.
17. 2 Chronicles 30:26.
18. 2 Chronicles 31:1.
19. 2 Chronicles 31:6–12.
20. 2 Chronicles 31:21.
21. 2 Kings 18:13–14.

> Let not Hezekiah deceive you for he shall not be able to deliver you out of his [Sennacherib's] hand: Neither let Hezekiah make you trust in the Lord, saying, The Lord will surely deliver us . . . Hath any of the gods of the nations delivered at all his land out of the hand of the king of Assyria? . . . Who are they among all the gods of the countries that have delivered their country out of mine hand, that the Lord should deliver Jerusalem out of mine hand?[22]

Hezekiah went immediately to the temple and called for the prophet Isaiah.[23] Isaiah told Hezekiah to "Be not afraid of the words which thou hast heard" and prophesied that the Lord would send the Assyrians away.[24]

In fact, Rab-shakeh departed to help Sennacherib fight a war on another front. However, Sennacherib sent a letter to Hezekiah warning him not to be deceived by the short reprieve, because he was surely coming to destroy Jerusalem. Hezekiah took the letter and "spread it before the Lord" in the temple.[25] He said:

> Of a truth, Lord, the kings of Assyria have destroyed the nations and their lands. And have cast their gods into the fire: for they were no gods, but the work of men's hands, wood and stone: therefore they have destroyed them. Now, therefore, O Lord our God, I beseech thee, save thou us out of his hand, that all the kingdoms of the earth may know that thou art the Lord God, even thou only.[26]

The Lord's response to Hezekiah is prophetic on several fronts: through Isaiah, the Lord prophesied that yet in the future, a remnant of the house of Judah would escape, return, and bear fruit.[27] But this did not mean that they would be taken by Assyria. As to that present situation, the Lord promised:

> Concerning the king of Assyria, he shall not come into this city, nor shoot an arrow there, nor come before it with shield, nor cast a bank

22. 2 Kings 18:28–35.
23. 2 Kings 19:1–2.
24. 2 Kings 19:6–8.
25. 2 Kings 19:9–14.
26. 2 Kings 19:17–19.
27. 2 Kings 19:30.

> against it. For I will defend this city, to save it, for mine own sake, and for my servant David's sake.[28]

The word of the Lord was fulfilled: during the night "an angel of the Lord went out and smote 185,000 Assyrian soldiers." Those who were left quickly departed.[29]

Judah had been protected from the Assyrians, but destruction was still on its way. Isaiah prophesied that because of future wickedness, Judah would be carried away captive by Babylon.[30] The prophecy was approximately a century away from being fulfilled.

Manasseh, Judah's Wicked King

Unfortunately, those who came to the throne after Hezekiah's death gave the prophecy little heed. In fact, Hezekiah's son, Manasseh, was the most evil king Judah ever had. Once again the temple was polluted by false images and altars to other gods.[31] Manasseh's reign is marked by bloodshed—including Isaiah's,[32] and Manasseh's own son that he sacrificed to the god Moloch.[33]

The scripture account says that Manasseh "seduced" his people "to do more evil than did the nations whom the Lord destroyed . . ."[34]

Under King Manasseh, the Lord declared, "Because Manasseh king of Judah hath done these abominations, and hath done wickedly . . . and hath made Judah to sin . . . I will wipe Jerusalem as a man wipeth a dish, wiping it, and turning it upside down."[35]

---

28. 2 Kings 19:32–34.
29. 2 Kings 19:35–36.
30. 2 Kings 20:17.
31. 2 Kings 21:2–5.
32. The story of Isaiah's martyrdom at the hands of Manasseh is recorded in both the Babylonian Talmud and the Jerusalem Talmud.
33. 2 Kings 21:9.
34. Ibid.
35. 2 Kings 21:11–13; 2 Chronicles 33:1–7.

Josiah's Religious Reform and Return to the Covenant

Judah had one "day" of light and glory remaining before the end. It came with Hezekiah's great-grandson Josiah.[36] He came to the throne and "began to seek after the God of David" at age eight, and began cleansing the temple and all the land at age twelve.[37]

During the cleansing of the temple, the priests discovered the book of the Law (scriptures). It had lain unused and unread for some time.[38] The king read the words of the book of the Law and tore his clothes with grief, "for great is the wrath of the Lord that is kindled against us, because our fathers have not hearkened unto the words of this book, to do according unto all this which is written concerning us."[39]

Josiah's fears of destruction were well founded. It was confirmed to him that the destruction *would* come, but because of his own righteousness, he would die in peace and not witness the annihilation of his people.[40]

Despite the dire prophecy, Josiah called all of his people "both small and great" to the temple.[41] With one last great effort, Josiah read the Law, or the covenant of the Lord, to the people.

> And the king stood by a pillar, and made a covenant before the Lord, to walk after the Lord, and to keep his commandments and his testimonies and his statutes with all their heart and all their soul, to perform the words of this covenant that were written in this book. And all the people stood to the covenant.[42]

After leading all of his people to renew their covenant with God, Josiah personally went throughout all the land of Israel to remove and destroy the idols, including the calves set up by Jeroboam so long

---

36. Accounts vary as to whether Josiah was the grandson or great-grandson of Hezekiah.
37. 2 Chronicles 34:3.
38. 2 Kings 22:8.
39. 2 Kings 22:11–13.
40. 2 Kings 22:14–20.
41. 2 Kings 23:2.
42. 2 Kings 23:3.

ago.[43] It is sobering to read the list of idols that were worshipped by the people and the list of those who claimed to have "familiar spirits" and false priesthood in serving those idols.

Again, we see a great Passover held. According to the chronicler, it was unlike any other.[44] Even considering Hezekiah's miraculous Passover celebration, it yet merits the praise that

> There was no passover like to that kept in Israel from the days of Samuel the prophet; neither did all the kings of Israel keep such a passover as Josiah kept, and the priests, and the Levites, and all Judah and Israel that were present.[45]
>
> And like unto him [Josiah] was there no king before him, that turned to the Lord with all his heart, and with all his soul, and with all his might, . . . neither after him arose there any like him.[46]

Josiah was killed at Megiddo (Armageddon) when Pharaoh Necho II went up against Babylon to aid Assyria.[47] Josiah was allied with Babylon and did not want to allow Pharaoh to march through his lands to attack his ally. Josiah's death destroyed the tenuous balance that Judah had attained in the international contest between empires.

"The Dying Time of the Kingdom of Judah"

When Josiah was killed at Megiddo in 609 BC, it was the beginning of the end for Judah and Jerusalem.

> Josiah was replaced by Jehoahaz, who was shortly taken into exile to Egypt and replaced by his brother Jehoiakim (609–587 BC). At the Battle of Carchemish in 605 BC, Babylon decisively defeated Assyria. Jehoiakim rebelled against Babylon, leading in 598 BC to an exile of selected Jews to Babylon. He was replaced by his son Jehoiachin, who was promptly exiled to Babylon after ruling only

---

43. 2 Kings 23:3–24.
44. 2 Kings 23:22.
45. 2 Chronicles 35:18.
46. 2 Kings 23:25.
47. 2 Kings 23:29–30; see "The Stunning Death of Judah's Most Righteous King," bible.ucg.org (or updated site ucg.org).

three months. The Babylonians next put Zedekiah, a son of Josiah, on the throne.[48]

The *Old Testament Student Manual* explains that

> The period between the death of Josiah and the final deportation of the Jews to Babylon could be described as the dying time of the kingdom of Judah. The cancer of idolatry was too deep in the hearts of the people for the surgery undertaken by Josiah to have any great effect. After Josiah, Judah began to deteriorate at an even greater rate than before. Nonetheless, spiritual surgeons were sent to proclaim the cure. "And the Lord God of their fathers sent to them by his messengers, rising up betimes and sending [his warnings]; because he had compassion on his people, and on his dwelling place" (2 Chron. 36:15). Indeed, the nearer the end came, the more voices were lifted up.[49]

Did Josiah Do Right in His Religious Reforms?

It's important to note that there is some ongoing controversy as to whether or not Josiah did right in his religious reforms, which included the destruction of the idols and the hilltop groves and places of worship.

Some scholars believe that a certain group of seventh century BC Levites/priests/lawyers referred to as *Deuteronomists* influenced the prophet Jeremiah, and through him, King Josiah. They believe that Jeremiah edited his own (and other) books to fit the doctrines put forth in the book of Deuteronomy, namely that 1) there was one God, Yahweh, of Israel, and He was the only God Israel should worship; 2) the place to worship Yahweh was in His temple, in Jerusalem; and 3) that Yahweh and Israel were bound by covenant, which if broken, certain consequences would follow.

These scholars state that the book of Deuteronomy was not written by Moses but rather written centuries later by the *Deuteronomists* to fit their ideals.

---

48. David R. Seely and JoAnn H. Seely, "Lehi and Jeremiah: Prophets, Priests, and Patriarchs."
49. "Judah's Return to Wickedness," *Old Testament Student Manual.*

Speculation as to whether King Josiah was influenced by this group to begin his religious cleansing of Israel still arises. The book of the "Law" found by the high priest Hilkiah during the temple cleansing and from which Josiah read is believed to have been the book of Deuteronomy.[50] Deuteronomy records Moses's last instructions to the Israelites and underscores their covenant relationship with God. They are strictly prohibited from worshipping the gods of the Canaanites, whose land they are going to possess. Several chapters are dedicated to the specific methods of worship that are forbidden and the blessings or cursings that will follow according to their faithfulness or rebellion.

Arguments still continue as to whether Josiah instigated a return to Israel's original covenant and religion or whether he brought about an ensuing destruction because he forbade them to worship the gods of the land and the idols they had brought into the temple itself.[51] William Hamblin writes:

> Some scholars believe the Deuteronomistic ideology was in fact an innovation of the late seventh century BC rather than representing an earlier ongoing sectarian movement within Israel whose ideas eventually crystallized into the Deuteronomistic books.

The fact that archaeological discoveries prove that Israel in fact did *not* maintain worship of one God—Yahweh—at His temple, provides weight to historian Margaret Barker's assertion that Israelites were not monotheistic and that Josiah, who many view as an enlightened and inspired reformer, was in fact a harsh dictator who disallowed freedom of religion.

The archeological finds demonstrate that the actions of the people negate the teachings that are recorded by their prophets. We cannot help but wonder how future archeologists will view our own worship practices.

William Hamblin states:

---

50. Peter C. Craigie, *The Book of Deuteronomy, New International Commentary on the Old Testament*; Robert I. Bradshaw, "Deuteronomy."
51. See Margaret Barker's "What Did King Josiah Reform?" and William Hamblin's "Vindicating Josiah," *Interpreter: A Journal of Latter-day Saint Faith and Scholarship,* 4, 165–76.

> We need to realize that the Deuteronomists represent Josiah's reforms as a restoration of the original pristine Mosaic temple theology. . . . For Barker, the Deuteronomist reforms were an apostate innovation which attempted to suppress the original authentic pre-exilic temple worship. . . . Why did Josiah believe these reforms were necessary? The fundamental problem was syncretism. The ancient Israelites were given numerous laws whose primary purpose was to distinguish them from non-Israelites. Circumcision, the types of clothing one could not wear, permitted hair styles, forbidden foods, marriage only to Israelites, and various cultic restrictions were all designed at least in part to prevent the Israelites from losing their distinct religious and ethnic identity. The reason the Jews survived the Babylonian captivity with their religion and identity relatively intact was precisely because of their refusal to syncretize with the culture and religion of their captors. The reason the Jews are one of the very few ancient Near Eastern peoples whose religion survives to the present is the restrictions on their syncretizing with foreign cultures and religions. Without Josiah's reforms, the Jews could probably not have survived the Babylonian captivity or Hellenistic and Roman occupations. They would have ended like the ten tribes of Israel, losing their identity in the captivity. There would have been no Judaism in the first century AD and hence no Jesus and no Christianity. Josiah's strict anti-syncretizing reforms of Israelite religious belief, practice, and cult insured the survival of the Jews. Centralization of Jewish worship in the Jerusalem temple was necessary because the provincial cultic sites were the major centers of cultic syncretism.[52]

Judah Conquered by Babylon

Although King Josiah turned his heart fully to God and completely destroyed all of the idols throughout the land and cleansed the temple, the heart of the people did not change with the heart of their king. Judah had a successive round of evil kings who, with the people, delighted in their apostate practices. The Lord removed His hand of

52. William Hamblin, "Vindicating Josiah," *Interpreter: A Journal of Latter-day Saint Faith and Scholarship*, 4, 165–76.

protection from Judah, and they, like the tribes to the north, were also taken captive, this time by Babylon.[53]

Babylon came three times against Judah, each time carrying away captives and treasure. The kings and the people were not humbled by these attacks but resented and stoned the prophets who spoke against them, including Jeremiah and Lehi.[54] Even the temple priests participated in the wickedness despite the fact that

> The Lord God of their fathers sent to them by his messengers . . . because he had compassion on his people, and on his dwelling place: But they mocked the messengers of God, and despised his words, and misused his prophets, until the wrath of the Lord arose against his people, till there was no remedy.[55]

With their final attack, the Babylonians carried away the last of the leading citizens, tore down the walls of Jerusalem, burned the temple, and carried away the last of its treasure.[56]

The land promised to Abraham was desolate of his children. They had polluted their inheritance and despised their birthright as covenant Israel. But the Lord was not finished in His work, and as He told His prophet Nephi: "I am God, and . . . I covenanted with Abraham that I would remember his seed forever."[57]

---

53. 2 Chronicles 33:11; 36:6–7, 10, 17–20.
54. Jeremiah 44:4–5; 1 Nephi 1:4, 13, 18–19.
55. 2 Chronicles 36:14–16.
56. 2 Chronicles 36:18–19.
57. 2 Nephi 29:14.

HISTORICAL CONTEXT

722 BC	Assyria Conquered Samaria/Israel/Ten Tribes
715 BC	Hezekiah—a Righteous King for Judah/Jerusalem
701 BC	Assyrian Sennacherib Conquered Philistia and Most of Judah; Threatens Jerusalem and the Lord Fights for Judah
609 BC	Babylon Conquered Assyria
587 BC	Babylon Conquered Jerusalem
539 BC	Medes/Persians Conquered Babylon
538/7 BC	Cyrus Allows Jews to Return to Jerusalem and Build Temple
530 BC	Cambysees (Cyrus's Son) Comes to Power
525 BC	Zerubbabel Begins Temple Building
522 BC	Darius I Becomes King
520 BC	Daniel Fasts and Prays for Jerusalem (Dan. 9:1–3)
520 BC	Haggai and Zechariah Prophesy in Jerusalem and Encourage the Building of the Temple to Proceed
515 BC	Temple Completed
486 BC	Queen Esther—Husband Ahasuerus (Xerxes)
465 BC	Artaxerxes I Becomes King
460s BC	Malachi Prophesies
445 BC	Nehemiah, the Cupbearer to King Artaxerxes, Becomes Governor of Jerusalem and Builds Walls of City
428 BC	Ezra the Scribe/Priest—Reads and Renews the Law and Covenant with the People and Encourages the Jews to Purify Themselves and Set Aside "Strange Marriages"

Dates are approximate. See Bible Dictionary, "Chronology," and S. Kent Brown and Richard Neitzel Holzapfel's *Between the Testaments: Malachi to Matthew.*

CHAPTER 13

Joseph in the New World: Branches over the Wall

JUST PRIOR TO HIS DEATH, FATHER LEHI, IN THE NEW WORLD, shared his final words and prophecies with his children. To his son Joseph, he said:

> For behold, thou art the fruit of my loins; and I am a descendant of Joseph who was carried captive into Egypt. And great were the covenants of the Lord which he made unto Joseph. Wherefore, Joseph truly saw our day. And he obtained a promise of the Lord that out of the fruit of his loins the Lord would raise up a righteous branch unto the house of Israel; not the Messiah, but a branch which was to be broken off, nevertheless, to be remembered in the covenants of the Lord that the Messiah should be made manifest unto them in the latter days, in the spirit of power, unto the bringing of them out of darkness unto light—yea, out of hidden darkness and out of captivity unto freedom.[1]

1. 2 Nephi 3:4–5.

Joseph's Patriarchal Blessing Promise: A Fruitful Bough

Before his death, Father Jacob (Israel) blessed each of his twelve sons with a patriarchal blessing that would hold true for each tribe throughout time. To Joseph, he said:

> Joseph is a fruitful bough, even a fruitful bough by a well; whose branches run over the wall . . . the blessings of thy father have prevailed above the blessings of my progenitors unto the utmost bound of the everlasting hills: they shall be on the head of Joseph, and on the crown of the head of him that was separate from his brethren.[2]

As we have discussed, Joseph's tribe of Ephraim and Manasseh were conquered and scattered by Assyria as part of the ten "lost" tribes. Ephraim had led the Northern Kingdom into apostasy and division from the tribes of Judah and Benjamin and any others who had moved to align themselves with those in Jerusalem. In the eyes of many, Israel was truly "lost," and the new national identity of the people who remained in the Jerusalem environs—regardless of their actual tribal lineage—became known as "the Jews," taking that name from the dominant ruling tribe of Judah.

For the most part, Judah retained their tribal identity and their relationship to covenant Israel because of their dedication and commitment to keeping sacred records, which included the holy texts (Torah, Tanakh, Holy Bible) and their genealogical records. Their response to being conquered and taken captive to Babylon differed from the lost tribes because of their adherence to the teachings of the prophets, which encouraged them to not assimilate into their new surroundings and to hold firm to the Law and the covenants of the fathers that set them apart as a peculiar people.

What, then, of the promises to Joseph and the other tribes? Were they null and void because they had departed from the Lord and forgotten the promises that had been given to their fathers?

We do not know the circumstances through which his family had found their way to living in Jerusalem, but there was a descendant of Joseph living in the south, in Jerusalem, at the time of the Babylonian

---

2. Genesis 49:22, 26.

conquest. Through him, one branch of Joseph was about to find its way out of the Old World and in to the New.

Lehi: From Jerusalem to the New World

Lehi received his call from the Lord in the first year of the reign of Zedekiah.[3] By that time, Babylon had already come against Jerusalem twice, taking captives each time.[4] The Babylonians had placed Zedekiah on the throne as a puppet-king, and the people of Jerusalem should have been greatly concerned. The Lord sent "many prophets" with the message that the people "must repent, or the great city Jerusalem must be destroyed,"[5] but the people hardly took note of the warnings. They stoned the prophets and placed Jeremiah in a pit to try to stop his voice.[6]

Lehi was struck by the words of Jeremiah and the others. He prayed to know the truth and received his own vision of the coming destruction.[7] He tried to share this knowledge with the people in Jerusalem, but they turned against him and tried to kill him.[8]

The Lord instructed Lehi to gather his family and to depart Jerusalem for the wilderness near the Red Sea. Although he was a wealthy man, he left everything behind in order to follow the Lord's instructions.[9] The response from his family was mixed: two sons followed in obedience, and two sons followed in anger and resentment, believing that their father was a foolish man and that he had harshly misjudged the people of Jerusalem. They did not believe that Jerusalem could, or would, be destroyed.[10]

After a grueling and dangerous ordeal in which Lehi's sons went back to Jerusalem to obtain plates of brass that contained the scriptures, the laws and covenants of the Lord, and their family genealogy,

---

3. 1 Nephi 1:4.
4. David R. Seely and JoAnn H. Seely, "Lehi and Jeremiah: Prophets, Priests, and Patriarchs."
5. 1 Nephi 1:4.
6. Jeremiah 38:6.
7. 1 Nephi 1:5–13.
8. 1 Nephi 1:20.
9. 1 Nephi 2:2–4.
10. 1 Nephi 2:11–13.

Lehi discovered that he was a descendant of Joseph of Egypt.[11] From thence forward, Lehi and his sons Nephi and Jacob continually reminded their posterity that they were a branch of Israel with an important work to do in fulfilling the promises of the Lord.

The Lord led Lehi and his family to the New World, where they established a civilization built upon the principles Israel had been taught in ancient times. They were a people of covenant, with a temple at the center of their society. Recognizing the importance of the plates of brass in preserving the truths upon which God would have them build, Lehi and those that followed after him were inspired to keep their own records to add to the testimony of the first. Those records are included in the Book of Mormon.

A Branch of Israel

Lehi's son Nephi established the purpose for their records from the very beginning of the Book of Mormon. They were not for keeping extensive histories or genealogies, but rather to remind their readers that they were of Israel, born of the early patriarchs and matriarchs who had made covenant promises with the Lord. Nephi did want to establish that they were a branch broken off from Israel, but his emphasis in that endeavor was on the covenant promises of the Lord to Israel and their duty to help bring about those promises.

> And now I, Nephi, do not give the genealogy of my fathers in this part of my record . . . for it sufficeth me to say that we are descendants of Joseph . . . for the fulness of mine intent is that I may persuade men to come unto the God of Abraham, and the God of Isaac, and the God of Jacob, and be saved.[12]

The need to remind their people that they were a branch of Israel is repeated frequently by various Book of Mormon prophets.[13] In fact, the Book of Mormon authors recognized early that they were likely not the only branch of Israel to be taken abroad. Jacob taught:

---

11. 1 Nephi 5:14–16.
12. 1 Nephi 6:1–2, 4.
13. 1 Nephi 15:12, 16; 1 Nephi 19:24; Jacob 2:25; Alma 26:36.

> And now, my beloved brethren, seeing that our merciful God has given us so great knowledge concerning these things, let us remember him, and lay aside our sins, and not hang down our heads, for we are not cast off; nevertheless, we have been driven out of the land of our inheritance; but we have been led to a better land, for the Lord has made the sea our path, and we are upon an isle of the sea. But great are the promises of the Lord unto them who are upon the isles of the sea; wherefore as it says isles, there must needs be more than this, and they are inhabited also by our brethren. For behold, the Lord God has led away from time to time from the house of Israel, according to his will and pleasure. And now behold, the Lord remembereth all them who have been broken off, wherefore he remembereth us also.[14]

At first the scattering of Israel must have felt like a curse and an exile from their beloved promised land, but as time passed, Lehi and his descendants came to realize and understand that they were part of God's plan to take the covenant promises of Israel throughout the world.

In remembering that they were of Israel, would they and their descendants be able to stay true to their covenants, or were they doomed to fail and fall into apostasy and forgetfulness as their ancestors had done?

The great allegory of the olive tree, recorded by Jacob early in the Book of Mormon, illustrates the story of God's love and care for Israel. A tender Gardener, he notices when branches begin to go wild and cuts and grafts them into other areas of His vineyard, hoping to restore them to health and strengthen the roots of Israel's covenant. The grafting includes joining Israelite blood to Gentile blood, intending that the roots and the branches grow together in balance. He offers the same tender care and nourishment to various branches, whether young, healthy, and strong, or old, decaying, and wild. The allegory reveals a God who will not give up, even when all who are assisting Him in the work feel hopeless. He continues to watch, dig, cut, and nourish until the tree is made whole. Years, decades, centuries,

14. 2 Nephi 10:20–22.

and millennia pass, but His work is not done until His people are restored.[15]

Joseph Fielding Smith wrote:

> Let us consider the fulfillment of this great promise and see how the nations of the earth, through Abraham's seed, have been blessed. First, the Lord always turns punishments to the accomplishments of his purposes. The scattering of the Israelites among all nations was a punishment inflicted upon them, but a great blessing extended to the nations among whom they were scattered.
>
> We see, then, how through the scattering of Israel, especially the descendants of the ten tribes who mingled with the Gentile nations, the blood of Abraham had been mixed with the blood of the Gentiles, and in this way the Gentiles have been brought into the seed of Abraham and are therefore entitled to receive, on conditions of their repentance, all the blessings promised to the seed of Abraham.[16]

Joseph Prophesies about His Descendants

We've seen that the patriarchal blessing given to Joseph was extensive and responsibility laden, matched only by that given to his brother, Judah. Those blessings and promises continue on through their posterity today.

In addition to Jacob's prophecy upon his family just before his death, Joseph also prophesied about the future of his posterity.

> And Joseph said unto his brethren, I die, and go unto my fathers; and I go down to my grave with joy. The God of my father Jacob be with you, to deliver you out of affliction in the days of your bondage; for the Lord hath visited me, and I have obtained a promise of the Lord, that out of the fruit of my loins, the Lord God will raise up a righteous branch out of my loins; and unto thee, whom my father Jacob hath named Israel, a prophet; (not the Messiah who is

15. See Jacob 5.
16. Joseph Fielding Smith, *The Restoration of All Things*, 129–37.

> called Shilo;) and this prophet shall deliver my people out of Egypt in the days of thy bondage.[17]
>
> And it shall come to pass that they shall be scattered again; and a branch shall be broken off, and shall be carried into a far country; nevertheless they shall be remembered in the covenants of the Lord, when the Messiah cometh; for he shall be made manifest unto them in the latter days, in the Spirit of power; and shall bring them out of darkness into light; out of hidden darkness, and out of captivity unto freedom.[18]

Joseph knew that his posterity would be scattered with branches broken off and taken to other countries. One of those branches, the family of Lehi, recognized and cherished their role as covenant keepers and covenant teachers in the New World. Lehi's son Jacob stated, "Wherefore, thus saith the Lord, I have led this people forth out of the land of Jerusalem, by the power of mine arm, that I might raise up unto me a righteous branch from the fruit of the loins of Joseph."[19]

In a future day, we will receive more records from each of the branches that have been broken off of the tree of Israel, including more from Joseph, Judah, and others.

The Lord has said:

> For I command all men, both in the east and in the west, and in the north, and in the south, and in the islands of the sea, that they shall write the words which I speak unto them; for out of the books which shall be written I will judge the world, every man according to their works, according to that which is written.
>
> For behold, I shall speak unto the Jews and the shall write it; and I shall also speak unto the Nephites and they shall write it; and I shall also speak unto the other tribes of the house of Israel, which I have led away, and they shall write it; and I shall also speak unto all nations of the earth and they shall write it.
>
> And it shall come to pass that the Jews shall have the words of the Nephites, and the Nephites shall have the words of the Jews; and the Nephites and the Jews shall have the words of the lost tribes

17. Genesis 50:24, Joseph Smith Translation.
18. Genesis 50:25, Joseph Smith Translation.
19. Jacob 2:25.

> of Israel; and the lost tribes of Israel shall have the words of the Nephites and the Jews . . . And I will show unto them that fight against my word and against my people, who are of the house of Israel, that I am God, and that I covenanted with Abraham that I would remember his seed forever.[20]

---

20. 2 Nephi 29:11–14.

CHAPTER 14

Judah in the New World

The Book of Mormon contains a brief account of a group of Jews who also escaped the Babylonian conquest of Jerusalem and found their way to the New World. They claimed to have come at the time when Zedekiah, king of Judah, was carried away captive into Babylon, which would put their departure very close to that of Lehi and his family.

Although they kept no records and therefore their history was handed down verbally, they claimed that their ancestors had left Jerusalem with King Zedekiah's son Mulek. John L. Sorenson reminds us that

> During the fall of the city or soon afterward, some Jews escaped, particularly to Egypt (Jeremiah was among the refugees), while others reached nearby Moab, Ammon and Edom. Zedekiah attempted to escape but was captured, and before Nebuchadrezzar, he saw his sons slain and then had his eyes put out before being taken to Babylon to captivity for the rest of his life.[1]

The Book of Mormon does not record the means by which Mulek and his companions escaped death or found their way to the Americas. John L. Sorenson wonders if they went first to Egypt with the main

1. John L. Sorenson, "The 'Mulekites.'"

body of Jews who left Jerusalem, or if they hired Phoenician mariners to transport them. Because they kept no written records, their path is unknown. Unlike Lehi who knew the importance of bringing the brass plates with him that contained the scriptures, the people of Mulek did not bring scriptural records, and by the time they were discovered by a group of Nephites led by Mosiah, they no longer believed in a creator or God.

Although they far outnumbered the people of Mosiah, these people, known as the "people of Zarahemla" or the *Mulekites*, eagerly joined with Mosiah and his people and elected Mosiah as their king. He caused them to be taught the language of the Nephites and the gospel of Christ.[2] Herein is one history where Judah and Joseph joined together as one in the covenant of God.

2. See Omni 1:14–19; Mosiah 25:2, 13–19; Helaman 8:21.

CHAPTER 15

Judah in Ireland?

In tracing the movements of the tribes of Joseph and of Judah, we cannot ignore the claims that have been made that Jeremiah, at the fall of Jerusalem, took Zedekiah's daughter, Tea Tephi, to safety in Ireland. There, according to legend, Tea Tephi was married to an Irish king, Heremon, and from their posterity eventually came the Stuart line in Scotland through which James I was enthroned in England. Thus, according to these legends, the British monarchy as we know it today is descended from the House of David and is a living part of the promise made to Judah and David so long ago.[1]

In addition, the legends assert that Jeremiah brought the ark of the covenant with him and buried it at the Hill of Tara. Further, it is believed that he also had in his care the very stone that Jacob used as a pillow on the evening he saw the angels ascending and descending to

1. See J. H. Allen's *Judah's Sceptre and Joseph's Birthright, An analysis of the Prophecies of the Scriptures in Regard to the Royal Family of Judah and the Many Nations of Israel, the Lost Ten Tribes*; Joseph Wild's *The Lost Ten Tribes and 1882*; and Frederick Robert Augustus Glover's *England, the Remnant of Judah and the Israel of Ephraim: The Two Families Under One Head; a Hebrew Episode in British History*.

heaven at Bethel.[2] This stone is believed to be the Stone of Scone, over which the kings of Britain are crowned.[3]

While some legends assert that Tea Tephi was actually the daughter of Pharaoh and numerous excavations of the Hill of Tara have been made in the attempt to find the ark, no one has found any artifacts or proof to satisfy scholars as to the validity of the stories. Although the story of Tea Tephi closely mirrors that of Mulek in the New World, all is really conjecture other than the truth that the king's daughters are mentioned as having survived in Jerusalem[4] and the remarkable fact that the British royal arms proudly boasts the lion and the unicorn—the symbols of the tribes of Judah and Joseph (Ephraim/Manasseh).[5]

---

2. See Genesis 28.
3. See J. H. Allen's *Judah's Sceptre and Joseph's Birthright, An analysis of the Prophecies of the Scriptures in Regard to the Royal Family of Judah and the Many Nations of Israel, the Lost Ten Tribes*; Joseph Wild's *The Lost Ten Tribes, and 1882*; Frederick Robert Augustus Glover's *England, the Remnant of Judah and the Israel of Ephraim: The Two Families Under One Head; a Hebrew Episode in British History*; Wikipedia's "Stone of Scone"; and Mairead Carew's *Tara and the Ark of the Covenant.*
4. Jeremiah 41:10.
5. Note that the unicorn has often been translated as the wild ox, which is the official symbol for Ephraim and Manasseh; see Deuteronomy 33:17.

CHAPTER 16

Those Who Were Left Behind in Judea

BABYLON LED THREE ATTACKS AGAINST JERUSALEM, EACH TIME taking prisoners away with them. The first conquest took Daniel and his friends as members of the royal household in order to prevent potential rebellion in behalf of a royal prince.[1] It is believed that in the second attack, Ezekiel, the priest, was taken captive. He ended up serving among the captives by the River Chebar.[2] With the final attack, the walls of Jerusalem were torn down, the temple was destroyed and burned, and the last noble or leading citizens were transported away.

Although the scriptural accounts may sound as if everyone was carried away captive at the fall of Jerusalem, the Biblical chroniclers tell us that "the poor of the land" were left to be vine dressers and husbandmen in Judea.[3] They also explain that Nebuchadnezzar appointed a Jewish governor to oversee the remnant who were left.[4] Gedaliah assured the Jews that remained that as long as they did not rebel, they would be treated fairly, and he encouraged them to till the land and

---

1. Daniel 1:1; "Daniel: Prophet of God, Companion of Kings," *Old Testament Student Manual.*
2. "Ezekiel: Watchman of Israel," *Old Testament Student Manual.*
3. 2 Kings 25:12; Jeremiah 39:10.
4. 2 Kings 25:22–23.

take care of it. At that time, many Jews who had been in hiding returned to their homes for the harvest.[5]

However, the uncertainty and chaos of the time is represented by the fact that although he was forewarned that his life was in danger, Gedaliah disregarded those warnings and was assassinated by a group of ten fellow Jews. They were led by a man named Ishmael who was from the royal family and had escaped the Babylonians. Ishmael and his friends did not stop their slaughter at Gedaliah's death but massacred others who had been supportive of Gedaliah and his efforts at bringing stability to Judea. They also decimated the nearby Babylonian garrison.[6]

Anarchy ensued following the death of Gedaliah, and the remaining Jewish leaders (including the murderers) seemed to have been particularly anxious about their safety and thought to go to Egypt for protection. They asked Jeremiah for counsel, and he told them that the Lord would have them stay in Judea. He warned them that famine and death would await them in Egypt, but they disregarded his counsel.[7] The scripture account indicates that this group forced Jeremiah and his scribe Baruch to go with them to Egypt,[8] and some traditions state that they later turned on Jeremiah and killed him there.[9] However, there are confused accounts of Jeremiah's last location, such as the legend of his presence in Ireland, considered in chapter 15.

While the land of Judea was not left entirely desolate, those that remained were not united politically or spiritually.

We have discussed the political conditions. In regard to the religious and spiritual climate, many still followed the false worship of Jehovah that had been set up by their ancestors. As an illustration of this spiritual confusion, it's of note to know that the specific group that went to Egypt despite Jeremiah's warning accused Jeremiah that they had been unlucky ever since they had stopped offering incense to the queen of heaven. The Asherah, or tree, or grove that was often associated with the queen of heaven (sometimes referred to as "god's

5. Jeremiah 40:7–12; see Nissan Mindei's "Gedaliah."
6. 2 Kings 25:25–26; Jeremiah 40:15–41.
7. Jeremiah 42; 43:1–7.
8. Jeremiah 43:5–9.
9. See Bible Dictionary, "Jeremiah."

wife") had been removed from the temple by King Josiah.[10] This would explain their particular animosity toward Jeremiah, who had encouraged Josiah to cleanse Judah from idolatry.

10. See Jeremiah 44:15–19; Daniel C. Peterson's "Nephi and His Asherah."

CHAPTER 17

Judah in Babylon

Jews in the Royal Courts of Babylon

When King Hezekiah of Jerusalem showed the Babylonians his treasure house, the prophet Isaiah chastised him and warned:

> Hear the word of the Lord of hosts: Behold the days are coming, when, all that is in your house, and that which your fathers have stored up this day, shall be carried to Babylon; nothing shall be left says the Lord. And some of your own sons, who are born to you, shall be taken away; and they shall be eunuchs in the palace of the king of Babylon.[1]

Isaiah's prophecy was fulfilled about 100 years later when Nebuchadnezzar brought his Babylonian armies against Jerusalem and carried its most notable citizens—together with the temple treasure—away to Babylon.

The ancient historian Josephus recorded:

> Now Nebuchadnezzar, king of Babylon, took some of the most noble of the Jews that were children, and the kinsmen of Zedekiah their king, such as were remarkable for their beauty of their bodies and comeliness of their countenances, and delivered them into the hands

1. Isaiah 39:5–7.

> of tutors . . . He also made some of them to be eunuchs . . . Now among these there were four of the family of Zedekiah, of the most excellent dispositions, the one of whom was called Daniel.[2]

Daniel's position as a young Jewish prince serving as a counselor (or wise man) in the court of the king in Babylon is unique in history, yet reveals a great deal about the relationship between the conquered Jewish people and their captors. While it is obvious that Nebuchadnezzar's officials believed that they could form Daniel and his friends into what they desired them to be, it does appear that there was a certain amount of autonomy and ability to speak freely and retain one's own values—as long as Daniel's counsel and interpretation of dreams proved valuable.

What is perhaps even more remarkable is the fact that Daniel and other Jewish captives remained in positions of responsibility within the inner court through successive Gentile kings representing different empires.[3] Daniel himself served under five kings: Nebuchadnezzar, Evil-merodach, Belshazzar, Darius, and Cyrus.[4]

Many wonder if Daniel might have presented Cyrus with Isaiah's prophecy given a century earlier that called Cyrus by name and instructed him to liberate the Jewish people.[5]

The fact that Daniel knew and honored prophecy is illustrated by his awareness of Jeremiah's prophecy that Judah would be captive to Babylon for seventy years.[6] Daniel had been studying Jeremiah's prophecy and pled with the Lord that the days of servitude might be accomplished and that Judah would obtain forgiveness for her sins and Jerusalem would be rebuilt.[7]

It is entirely conceivable that Daniel would be quick to supply Cyrus with the Isaiah scroll that called the king by name:

---

2. Flavius Josephus, *Antiquities of the Jews*, 18.186–89.
3. See "Daniel: Prophet of God, Companion of Kings," *Old Testament Student Manual.*
4. Ibid.
5. Isaiah 44:24–45:7.
6. Jeremiah 25:11–12; 29:10.
7. Daniel 9:1–2, 16–19; see Ross E. Winkle's "Jeremiah's Seventy Years for Babylon: A Re-Assessment, Part I: The Scriptural Data," 201–14.

> Thus saith the LORD thy redeemer, and he that formed thee from the womb, I am the LORD that maketh all things; that stretcheth forth the heavens alone; that spreadest abroad the earth by myself . . . That confirmeth the word of his servant, and performeth the counsel of his messengers; that saith to Jerusalem, Thou shalt be inhabited; and to the cities of Judah, Ye shall be built, and I will raise up the decayed places thereof . . .
>
> That saith of Cyrus, He is my shepherd, and shall perform all my pleasure: even saying to Jerusalem, Thou shalt be built; and to the temple, Thy foundation shall be laid. Thus saith the Lord to his anointed, to Cyrus, whose right hand I have holden, to subdue nations before him; and I will loose the loins of kings, to open before him the two leaved gates; and the gates shall not be shut; I will go before thee, and make the crooked places straight: I will break in pieces the gates of brass, and cut in sunder the bars of iron: And I will give thee the treasures of darkness, and hidden riches of secret places, that thou mayest know that I, the LORD, which call thee by thy name, am the God of Israel. For Jacob my servant's sake, and Israel mine elect, I have even called thee by thy name: I have surnamed thee, though thou hast not known me. I am the LORD, and there is none else, there is no God beside me: I girded thee, though thou hast not known me.[8]

Babylon fell to Cyrus and the Medes and Persians in 550 BC, thirty-seven years after Jerusalem had fallen to Babylon.[9] Nebuchadnezzar had been right to worry about what would happen to his kingdom;[10] empires rose and fell in quick succession—and the Jews remained within their borders in a relatively beneficial relationship on both sides. That relationship is particularly illustrated by the fact that once Cyrus allowed the Jews to return to their homeland in 538 BC and even encouraged them to rebuild their temple, the majority of the Jews chose to remain within the boundaries of the territory of the former Babylonian empire. They were thriving. Even in the worst of times, when persecution against the Jews arose in 479–73 BC, Esther's

8. Isaiah 44:24–45:4.
9. See Renald Showers's "Babylon and Medo-Persia."
10. See Daniel 2.

close relative, Mordecai, was appointed as the closest advisor to the king,[11] and King Artaxerxes appointed his own Jewish cupbearer to become the governor of Jerusalem in 444 BC.[12]

The *Old Testament Student Manual* states that

> Life in captivity was not necessarily one of horror or slavery. The Jews were given a good deal of social freedom and economic opportunity. They proved to be enterprising in business and economic affairs, a gift valued by the Babylonians. The Babylonian Jews were allowed to move about freely, and to live in their communities within or near the great cities, and to carry on their way of life. In fact, so secure was their life in Babylon that when Cyrus allowed the captive people to return to Judah to rebuild the temple seventy years later, many of them refused to leave Babylon.[13]

Lessons Learned: The Jews Put Away Idol Worship, Focus on the Scriptures

Unlike their northern brothers who had been carried into captivity and assimilated, the majority of the Jews viewed the destruction of Jerusalem and the temple as a confirmation of the warning voices of the prophets who had chastised them for their idolatry. This seems to have resulted in a wholehearted repentance and determination to never repeat their mistake again. Rather, they reinforced their walls of faith with an emphasis on keeping the Law of God and of teaching that Law to their children. Although the ten tribes of the north completely forgot their heritage, the Jews honored and revered their history and the inheritance of faith that had been passed down from Abraham and Sarah. Despite persecution, they held firm through the many conquerors who sought to subdue them and force them to repudiate their religion. Through the prophet Nephi, the Lord assured that He remembered His "ancient covenant people" the Jews and encouraged his readers to "remember the travails, and the labors, and

11. Esther 10:2–3.
12. Nehemiah 2, 6.
13. "The Lasting Effects of the Fall and Captivity of Judah," *Old Testament Student Manual.*

the pains of the Jews, and their diligence unto me, in bringing forth salvation unto the Gentiles."[14]

One of the most notable ways in which the Jews "through their diligence, brought forth salvation to the Gentiles" was through their love of the scriptural records. Prior to the Babylonian captivity, the scriptures were not widely known and understood among the general population. But with the reforms required to be true as God's covenant people, the Jews recognized the importance of gathering the scriptures together and in teaching them throughout their congregations and families. Not only was the written word precious, but many commentators and religious groups added their own oral interpretations or commentaries on the scriptures as well so that both the written and oral laws became of great value to the people.

As the scriptures took on new importance, the prophets who had written them also took on a new honored status. As the Jews watched Isaiah's prophecy to Cyrus be fulfilled, for example, their reverence for Isaiah increased. Daniel showed faith in Jeremiah's prophecy of a seventy-year banishment, and the Jews were counting the years to prove the prophecy true. In addition, readers recognized the various warnings that had been recorded over the centuries—warnings that had been ignored but were now fulfilled in their own captivity.

Richard D. Draper wrote:

> Judah's prophets kept her faith from extinction and her culture from decay. They did this, in part, by reminding her of her unique relation to her God and the mission He had assigned her. The prophets also fueled the Jews' desire to return to their own land, rebuild God's temple, and once more become His people. Further, these inspired men facilitated the miracle by satisfactorily answering the exile's most urgent questions and, in the process, giving the Jews both hope and direction.[15]

Finally, the *Old Testament Student Manual* explains that

> Although the Jews have been scattered geographically since the exile in Babylonia, they have been kept united religiously through the

14. 2 Nephi 29:4–5.
15. Richard D. Draper, "The Prophets of the Exile; Saviors of a People," 245–65.

> institutions that developed out of the exile. One of these institutions is the synagogue. The fact that the Nephites had synagogues suggests that they were important in worship in Judah before the exile (see for example 2 Nephi 26:26). Some Jewish scholars claim the synagogue goes back to Moses, but most place its emergence in Babylon, and it seems likely that it at least grew in importance at that time. According to the *Encyclopedia Judaica*, "the Exiles, deprived of the Temple, in a strange land, feeling the need for consolation in their distress, would meet from time to time, probably on Sabbaths, and read the Scriptures" (s.v. "synagogue," 15:579–80). The word *synagogue* means "assembly," though often it is used to mean the building. In fact, there is reason to believe that for many years before buildings were erected, the Jews assembled in the streets to hear the scriptures read and translated. Thus it is the people, or the assembly, that is the real synagogue.[16]

The Jews in Babylon refused to let go of their religious convictions, and thus, became set apart from the general population of the communities they inhabited. From the time of the Babylonian conquest, the Jews settled in various areas of the world, including Alexandria, Athens, Rome, Barcelona, and London. In each of those capitals, they retained their own distinct identity, and formed a community built around their synagogue and their scriptures. Of the twelve original tribes of Israel, the Jews are the only ones who still remember and cherish their tribal identity as children of Israel.

16. "The Lasting Effects of the Fall and the Captivity of Judah," *Old Testament Student Manual*, 261; see also Robert I. Bradshaw's "The Babylonian Exile of Israel."

CHAPTER 18

Judah: The First Return to Judea and the Building of the Temple

CHRONOLOGY of the TEN TRIBES and JUDAH

722 BC	Assyria Conquered Samaria/Israel/Ten Tribes
715 BC	Hezekiah—a Righteous King for Judah/Jerusalem
701 BC	Assyrian Sennacherib Conquered Philistia and Most of Judah; Threatens Jerusalem and the Lord Fights for Judah
609 BC	Babylon Conquered Assyria
587 BC	Babylon Conquered Jerusalem
539 BC	Medes/Persians Conquered Babylon
538/7 BC	**Cyrus** Allows Jews to Return to Jerusalem and Build Temple
530 BC	Cambysees (Cyrus's Son) Comes to Power
525 BC	**Zerubbabel** Begins Temple Building
522 BC	Darius I Becomes King
520 BC	**Daniel** Fasts and Prays for Jerusalem (Dan. 9:1–3)
520 BC	**Haggai** and **Zechariah** Prophesy in Jerusalem and Encourage the Building of the Temple to Proceed
515 BC	Temple Completed
486 BC	Queen **Esther**—Husband Ahasuerus (Xerxes)
465 BC	Artaxerxes I Becomes King
460s BC	**Malachi** Prophesies

445 BC	**Nehemiah**, the Cupbearer to King Artaxerxes, Becomes Governor of Jerusalem and Builds Walls of City
428 BC	**Ezra** the Scribe/Priest—Reads and Renews the Law and Covenant with the People and Encourages the Jews to Purify Themselves and Set Aside "Strange Marriages"

Dates are approximate. See Bible Dictionary, "Chronology," and S. Kent Brown and Richard Neitzel Holzapfel's *Between the Testaments: Malachi to Matthew*.

Zerubbabel and Joshua—The First to Return and Lay the Foundation

Even as they had left Jerusalem in various waves of conquest, so those Jews who elected to return to Jerusalem returned in various waves of pilgrimage. Their return to their homeland was purely voluntary. It is touching to read the stories of the individuals involved who, though seemingly small and unimportant (one being a cupbearer to the king in Persia), were known and called by the Lord to help in His work and to minister to His people.

Cyrus, of whom Isaiah had prophesied of nearly 175 years before his reign, not only issued a decree in 537 BC that the Jews were free to return to Jerusalem, but he also provided them funds to rebuild their temple. He even returned the treasure that had been taken from the temple by the Babylonians.[1]

However, not many Jews responded to Cyrus's release, and few returned to Jerusalem. Most elected to stay in Babylonia. They became known as the Jews of the *Diaspora* or dispersion.

The first group of returning exiles arrived in Judea sometime after 536 BC under the leadership of Zerubbabel, a member of the royal Davidic line,[2] and Joshua (or Jeshua), a Levite priest of the lineage of Zadok. (Zadok was the high priest at the dedication of Solomon's temple.) According to Ezra, 42,360 people departed Babylon for Jerusalem with the first group. Their servants numbered 7,367 for a total of just under 50,000 people.[3]

1. Ezra 1:1–3, 6–8.
2. 1 Chronicles 3:19.
3. Ezra 2:64–65.

The first religious act performed by the returning pilgrims was to dedicate an altar to the Lord. It was the seventh month, noted for the celebration of the Feast of Trumpets, the Day of Atonement, and the Feast of Tabernacles.[4] From that point forward, the daily sacrifices were offered even though the foundation of the temple was not laid; however, money was sent to purchase cedar trees from Lebanon for its future building.[5]

When the temple foundation was laid a year later,

> [Many of the] ancient men, that had seen the first house, when the foundation of this house was laid before their eyes, wept with a loud voice; and many shouted for joy; so that the people could not discern the noise of the shout of joy from the noise of the weeping of the people: for the people shouted with a loud shout, and the noise was heard afar off.[6]

Trouble with the Samaritans

Trouble with the Samaritans from central Israel began shortly after the foundation of the temple was laid. The Samaritans came to Zerubbabel and said, "Let us build with you: for we seek your god, as ye do; and we do sacrifice unto him since the days of Esar-haddon king of Assur, which brought us up hither."[7]

What the Samaritans meant in stating that they were seeking the god of Israel (since the days of the king of Assur) is that they had been foreigners transported to the land of Israel by the Assyrians, just as the Assyrians had transported the native ten tribes *out* of the land. When the newcomers arrived, they were tormented by lions and felt that their struggles must be because they were not worshipping the god of the new land and he was rebuking them for their oversight. They reached out to the Assyrian king through their leaders, and he sent them priests who had formerly dwelt in the Northern Kingdom to teach them about the god of Israel. Unfortunately, the ten tribes had been apostate for generations, so the teachings of the priests were

---

4. Ezra 3:1, 4; see Lynda Cherry's *The Feasts and Festivals of the Messiah*.
5. Ezra 3:6–7.
6. Ezra 3:12–13.
7. Ezra 4:1–2.

undoubtedly a conglomerate of religious practices and teachings that supposedly represented Jehovah but in fact strayed from the strictness of the covenant.[8]

Prior to the request of the Samaritans to help build the temple, the Jews had already viewed the Samaritan people as corrupt. The Samaritans (capital of the Northern Kingdom of Israel) had turned to calf worship as set up by Jeroboam and later worshipped many other idols. King Ahab and his Queen Jezebel had ruled in Samaria and were considered to be the most wicked rulers Israel had ever known.

Those people of Samaria who remained in the land after the Assyrian conquest had intermarried with the foreigners who had been brought in to replace the larger population. This intermarriage was seen as further corruption of the covenant by the Jews, and they would not allow the Samaritans to help rebuild the temple when they made the offer. From that time forward, there was constant discord as the Samaritans hampered the building of the temple by sending letters to the kings of Persia accusing the Jews of rebellion and by throwing stones at the workers as they attempted to build the temple and the city walls. For a time, the building on the temple ceased.[9]

The Prophets Haggai and Zechariah Encourage Temple Building

Haggai was a prophet sent to prophesy and encourage the people at Jerusalem in their temple building. The building of the temple had been sporadic at best with the people stopping for long periods of time to see to their crops and their own houses. They had begun to justify themselves by saying, "[Now] just isn't the right time to build the Lord's house."[10]

Haggai chastised them: "Is it time for you, O ye, to dwell in your ceiled houses, and this house lie waste? Now therefore thus saith the Lord of hosts; Consider your ways."[11]

---

8. 2 Kings 17:24–29.
9. Ezra 4:11–24.
10. Haggai 1:2.
11. Haggai 1:4–5.

The people had been sowing but brought in little to eat. They were truly destitute. The Lord, through Haggai, told them that if they would finish the temple, the blessings they sought would be poured out upon them. The Lord encouraged:

> Yet now be strong, O Zerubbabel, saith the Lord; and be strong, O Joshua, the high priest; and be strong, all ye people of the land, saith the Lord, and work: for I am with you, saith the Lord of hosts. The glory of this latter house shall be greater than of the former, saith the Lord of hosts: and in this place will I give peace, saith the Lord of hosts.[12]

Zechariah was a prophet sent about the same time as Haggai to also encourage the people to build the temple. He prophesied:

> Thus saith the Lord: I am returned to Jerusalem with mercies: my house shall be built in it.[13]

> The hands of Zerubbabel have laid the foundation of this house: his hands shall also finish it; and thou shalt know that the Lord of hosts hath sent me.[14]

The temple was finished in 515 BC, approximately twenty years after the first pilgrims from Babylon made their way to Jerusalem. This temple is known as the second temple, or the temple of Zerubbabel. It was but a pale shadow of the first built by Solomon. According to the Bible Dictionary:

> The Jews reckoned the temple of Zerubbabel to be in five points inferior to the temple of Solomon: in the absence of (1) the Ark of the Covenant (lost or burned at the destruction of Jerusalem and never renewed); (2) the Schechinah or manifestation of the glory of the Lord; (3) the Urim and Thummim; (4) the holy fire upon the altar; (5) the spirit of prophecy.[15]

---

12. Haggai 2:4, 9.
13. Zechariah 1:16.
14. Zechariah 4:9.
15. Bible Dictionary, "Temple of Zerubbabel."

James E. Talmage adds:

> It is known in history as the Temple of Zerubbabel. In general plan it was patterned after the Temple of Solomon, though in many of its dimensions it exceeded its prototype. The court was divided into a section for priests only and another for public; according to Josephus the division was effected by a wooden railing. An altar of unhewn stone was erected in place of the great brazen altar of old. The Holy Place was graced by but one candlestick [Menorah] instead of ten; and by a single table for the shew-bread instead of the ten tables overlaid with gold which stood in the first Temple. We read also of a golden altar of incense, and of some minor appurtenances. The Most Holy Place was empty, for the Ark of the Covenant had not been known after the people had gone into captivity.[16]

Nehemiah Builds City Walls, and Ezra the Priest Renews the Covenant

There is a span of about three generations between the first group of refugees to Jerusalem and the arrival of Nehemiah (about 445 BC) and Ezra (about 428 BC). During this period, Persian culture reached its greatest height.

Nehemiah was a royal cupbearer in the Persian court to King Artaxerxes. When he heard news that the people in Jerusalem were faring poorly and that the walls of Jerusalem were still broken down and the gates not restored, Nehemiah took it personally. "It came to pass, when I heard these words, that I sat down and wept, and mourned certain days, and fasted and prayed before the God of heaven."[17]

When the king saw the sadness upon his courtier's face, he inquired the reason, and Nehemiah implored the king to allow him to go to Jerusalem and help to build it.[18] The king not only allowed the request but also appointed Nehemiah as governor of the province

16. James E. Talmage, *House of the Lord: A Study of Holy Sanctuaries Ancient and Modern.*
17. Nehemiah 1:3–4.
18. Nehemiah 2:5.

of Judea. In addition, he instructed that gold and silver be sent with Nehemiah to help in the work.

> Nehemiah's energy, ability, unselfish patriotism, and personal integrity brought a new, exuberant Judah into existence once again. The restoration of Jerusalem, which had lain in ruins for a century and a half, was begun.[19]

Nehemiah led the way in restoring the city walls and gates and in beautifying the temple. Much of this work was done with the laborers bearing weapons to protect themselves against the Samaritans, who continually interfered with the work.

Ezra arrived in Jerusalem at approximately the same time as did Nehemiah. Ezra was a scribe/priest who had it in his heart to worship at the temple. Once again, Artaxerxes sent support with gold and silver to help with the building process. He went further in instructing Ezra to appoint magistrates and judges and to teach the Law of the Lord to those that did not know it.[20]

Ezra worked in conjunction with Nehemiah to help restore Judah to its former strength.

When Ezra arrived in Jerusalem, he was dismayed to learn that many of the people—princes, as well as priests—had intermarried with the foreign idol-worshipping people of the land. "And when I heard this thing, I rent my garment and my mantle, and plucked off the hair of my head and of my beard, and sat down astonished."[21] He told the Lord that he blushed with shame to ask for His help and blessings upon a people who continued to repeat the same mistakes of old.

After Ezra "confessed the sins" of the people before the Lord, he sat down before the temple, and "there assembled unto him out of Israel a very great congregation of men and women and children: for the people wept very sore."[22]

---

19. "Builder of Walls and Wills (Nehemiah)," *Old Testament Student Manual.*
20. Ezra 7:25.
21. Ezra 8:3.
22. Ezra 10:1.

There followed a time of confession, forsaking of sins, and cleansing as has no comparison in the scriptures: The people literally sat in the street before the temple and wept for their sins. It seems fitting that it was raining, for it seemed that all the heavens wept with the people. They came forward and offered and covenanted that they would "put aside" their "strange wives" and keep covenant. There had been so many who had intermarried that it took several weeks for each to come forward, confess, and covenant.[23] We can only assume that as with Ruth, the Gentile who married Boaz, any wives who were willing to convert and accept the covenant and have Israel's God to be their god would have been fully accepted into that covenant.

It helps to understand the context of the timing of Ezra's reading of the Law (or covenant and scriptures) to the people and their outpouring of confession and repentance. According to the account in Ezra, this event took place in the ninth month,[24] but Nehemiah records a very similar event of Ezra reading the Law to the people as taking place during the seventh month.[25] Perhaps Ezra read the Law to the people on two occasions (or more), but if the date as recorded in Nehemiah is correct, then it would have begun on the first day of the seventh month. This is important, because that date commemorates the Feast of Trumpets, a time to "wake up" and ponder one's standing before God. Ten days later, the Day of Atonement would occur, where one's name was written in the Book of Life or the Book of Death. The Feast of Trumpets heralded a ten-day period of repentance in order to prepare oneself to stand before the Lord and be found acceptable on the most sacred Day of Atonement. Following five days after the Day of Atonement is the Feast of Tabernacles, the most joyous day that commemorates the Lord's care of the children of Israel in the Sinai desert but also foreshadows the great day of the gathering of Israel unto the Lord.[26]

---

23. Ezra 10:9, 17.
24. Ezra 10:9.
25. See Nehemiah 8.
26. See Lynda Cherry's *The Feasts and Festivals of the Messiah*.

Ezra and Nehemiah had to remind the Israelites who Israel was by reminding them who Israel was unto God. They were beloved and had inherited many promises because of their righteous forebears, but there were also high expectations that came with the covenant, including the importance of raising whole families within its sacred bounds.

CHAPTER 19

Judea between the Testaments

At the close of the Old Testament, the only remaining tribe of Israel that can be tracked is Judah, or *the Jews*. The ten tribes of the Northern Kingdom of Israel had long before been carried away by Assyria to other lands. Benjamin, too, became lost or assimilated as they dwelt among their Jewish brethren. Although the identity of the other tribes was lost as they were swallowed up and mixed among the peoples of other nations, the Jews maintained a strong sense of identity in captivity and afterward. In fact, their captivity in Babylon seemed to cement a sense of nationality and pride as the people of the Lord Jehovah.

The Old Testament books of Haggai, Zechariah, Malachi, Nehemiah, and Ezra record a partial history of the Jews after they were given the freedom to return to Jerusalem. That history takes us only through about 432 BC. What happened between that time and the day that Zacharias stood before the veil in the temple and was visited by the angel Gabriel?[1]

Many significant events occurred in world history during the intervening centuries. Empires rose and fell in a steady cadence that perfectly matched Daniel's prophecies.[2] Each left its mark on the

1. Luke 1:5–13.
2. Daniel 2, 5, 7, 8, 11.

Jewish people and created ripples that would help form the society into which Jesus was born.

The Conquering Empires of the Old World

Persia defeated Babylon and had been the reigning power for about one hundred years by the time the Old Testament era closed. Median-Persian kings that had influence on the Jewish people included

- **Cyrus**, who allowed the Jews to return to their homeland and rebuild their temple, about 537 BC.
- **Darius**, who reluctantly sent Daniel into the lion's den and also encouraged and supported the Jewish people in rebuilding their temple and city, 522 BC.
- **Ahasuerus (or Xerxes)**—Esther's husband; we have no records of Ahasuerus' involvement with the temple or Jerusalem, but he did allow the Jews to protect themselves against Haman's diabolical plan, and he also appointed Mordecai to a position of great importance as his counselor.
- **Artaxerxes**, who encouraged and financed the efforts of his cupbearer Nehemiah, whom he appointed to be the first governor of Jerusalem (445 BC), and Ezra, the scribe/priest who helped unify and recommit the people of Jerusalem to the Law (428 BC). Artaxerxes also instructed Ezra to appoint magistrates and judges in Jerusalem and to teach the laws of God unto any who did not know them.[3]

In 334 BC, **Alexander the Great** (Greece) attacked and defeated the Persian Empire. He quickly swept through and conquered the entire Middle East. He conquered Jerusalem in 332 BC. The leading citizens of Jerusalem, led by the temple high priest, sent representatives to Alexander asking that the city be spared from destruction. He granted the request and, it is said, appreciated the intelligence, industriousness, and steadiness of the Jews. However, the Jewish people were

3. Ezra 7:25.

about to face the greatest challenge yet presented: the *Hellenization*, or the spread of Greek culture throughout the world.

Hellenization

> The Greeks were sure that their culture held the solution to the world's problems. It was their goal, at least initially, to convert the youth of the world to a classical Greek viewpoint. To accomplish this objective, they established cities where learning was to take place uninhibited by old customs. As a result, Greek became the new language of the empire and the Hellenic culture became the standard. Greeks looked on the traditions, customs, and religion of the Jews as primitive, archaic, and barbaric; they set about to "enlighten" them. Even the surrounding peoples quickly accepted the Greek rule, and soon the Jews were an island in a sea of Greek influence. The crucial question arose about whether, against the force of this united front, the Jewish nation could hold its own or whether it would be subsumed culturally and religiously as it had been politically and thus lose its identity.[4]

The Greek conquest of Jerusalem was through the mind, particularly of the youth. The Greeks, recognizing they could retain power more easily if they swayed Jewish youth to their viewpoint, used the gymnasium to break down Jewish thought and tradition. The gymnasium was one of the mightiest symbols of the Hellenization of Judah. The gymnasium was more than an athletic club. It was a school for boys with a curriculum consisting entirely of Greek learning, with emphasis on Greek classical literature and a strong emphasis on sports. "The word *gymnasium* comes from the Greek word *gymnos*, which means 'naked.' The Greeks glorified the beauty of the human body and had the young men in the gymnasiums participate in athletic contests in the nude."[5]

While conservative Jews looked upon the practices of the gymnasium as an abomination, many from the higher class families embraced it. In fact, many wealthy families began to refrain from having their sons circumcised, or the young men underwent painful surgeries

---

4. "Between the Testaments," *Old Testament Student Manual*.
5. Ibid.

to hide the token of the Abrahamic covenant since their circumcision distinguished them from other Greeks.

It is important to understand that from the time of their captivity by Babylon, most Jews lived outside of Palestine.

> Life in captivity was not necessarily one of horror or slavery; rather, the Jews were given a good deal of social freedom and economic opportunity. They proved to be enterprising in business and economic affairs. They were allowed to move about freely, to live in their communities within or near the great cities, and to carry on their way of life.[6]

In fact, the largest population of Jews lived in Alexandria, Egypt. The Jewish people were dispersed throughout the empire. The term for dispersed or scattered Israel is *Diaspora*, meaning "the dispersion."

Persecution and Desecration of the Temple

Following Alexander's death, his generals fought for control of his empire.

Two of the generals finally gained control of the Holy Land. Seleucus conquered Syria and the northern part of the Middle East. Ptolemy took Egypt. Palestine lay directly between the two rivals. The Holy Land changed hands several times during the next few years as **Ptolemies** and **Seleucids** fought for its control, causing disastrous results to the towns and population of Judea. In 301 BC it finally fell to the Ptolemies of Egypt, to whom it belonged for one hundred years. While under the control of the Ptolemies, the Jews enjoyed relative religious and cultural freedoms. However, Judea remained a point of contention between the two rival powers. It was not until 200 BC that the Seleucids were able to capture and hold Judea.[7]

Terrible sorrow and persecution came to the Jewish people when **Antiochus IV**, a Seleucid king, came to power in 175 BC. He was determined to destroy the religion of the Jews, hoping thus to bring them into a submissive and easily governed people. He built a gymnasium in Jerusalem and plundered and desecrated the temple. He

---

6. Bernhard W. Anderson, *Understanding the Old Testament*, 376.
7. See "Between the Testaments," *Old Testament Student Manual.*

established a garrison fortress near the Temple Mount to insure that his orders were carried out: sabbath observance, celebration of the holy days, and circumcision were forbidden on pain of death. He sent soldiers throughout villages, and if a child was found circumcised, it was killed, hung about its mother's neck, and the mother hurled off a high wall. He forced the priests to sacrifice swine upon the holy altar and killed any who would not comply.

The Maccabees

The persecution carried out by Antiochus IV united the Jewish people in the spirit of rebellion. In 167 BC, a priest from the **Asmonean (Hasmonean)** family named **Mattathias** refused to offer a sacrifice to a pagan god when ordered to do so. When another priest stepped forward to offer the sacrifice, Mattathias grabbed a sword and killed both the priest and the Syrian officer. Mattathias and his five sons then fled to the hills and called on all of Judah to join them. "All who are zealous for the sake of the Torah, who uphold the covenant, march out after me!"[8]

Although Mattathias died shortly afterward, his sons carried on the work of leading the Jewish people in rebellion against their Seleucid overlords. **Judah Maccabee**, or **Judas Maccabeus**, the son of Mattathias, is known as "[God's] hammer" because of his skills in warfare. Leading the vastly outnumbered and under-supplied Jewish people in guerrilla forays, Judah successfully recaptured Jerusalem, and the temple was cleansed and rededicated in 164 BC. This dedication took place on the third anniversary of its desecration by Antiochus. It was during this rededication that the miracle of the eight days of light from an inadequate source of oil found in a temple lamp resulted in the commemorative festival called **Hanukkah**. Judas found only one cruse of pure olive oil that still bore the seal of the high priest. He needed the oil to light the Menorah in the Holy Place, but the one cruse was sufficient for one day only. Miraculously, it burned for eight days until new supplies could be found.

8. 1 Maccabees 2:27–28; see bible.usccb.org.

Upon Judah's death, his brother Jonathan was chosen by the people to lead them in the war against the Seleucids. The Jewish people revered and honored the Maccabean, or Hasmonean family, and the family quickly rose to power. Jonathan became not only their military leader, but in a move for reconciliation, the new Seleucid king appointed Jonathan as the new high priest in Jerusalem. Their brother, Simon, followed in their footsteps as commander and high priest and was finally able to dislodge the foreigners and Jewish Hellenists from the fortress at the Temple Mount in 142 BC, thus creating a free Jewish state for the first time in 440 years.

Unfortunately, within a short time, the Hasmonean family was following in the footsteps of the elite who had preceded them: selling their integrity for favors and prestige. By the time of Aristobulus's rule, the family had taken the title of "king" for themselves, as well as being the commanders of the army *and* the high priest. The Hasmonean/Maccabean family successfully launched campaigns to expand the borders of their nation, attempting to bring its boundaries back to the time of King David. Along the way, they forced or coerced the Gentiles within their borders to convert to Judaism . . . including the Idumeans, from whom Herod the Great was to come. As the Hasmonean family continued to degenerate, they began to fight amongst themselves for power. Two brothers, Hyrcanus II and Aristobulus II, had a protracted battle that brought about civil war for their country. They sent to Rome for help in ending the dispute, and by doing so, effectively brought Jewish independence to an end.

Judea under Rome

In 164 BC, Judah Maccabee had made an alliance with Rome, requesting help to overthrow the Seleucid government. The alliance was renewed with the successive Hasmonean leaders. The **Romans**, however, did not arrive to rule Judea until 63 BC, when **Pompey** took control of it for Rome.

When Pompey took control of Palestine for Rome, he entered the temple in Jerusalem:

> Surrounded by lieutenants, Pompey walked into the courtyard and passed into the area of the temple proper. He entered where it was unlawful for gentiles to walk. Without pomp or ceremony, he continued into the Holy Place, strode across the room, and stood before the veil of the temple, which separated this room from the Holy of Holies, one of the most sacred spaces in the world for the Jews. He paused briefly, parted the curtain with his hand, and walked into the room, a place reserved for the high priest on the Day of Atonement. The room was empty. After a brief pause, Pompey turned around and left the sanctuary as quickly as he had entered it. Evidently, he did not take any of the furnishings or rob the treasury. On the following day, he commanded the priests to cleanse the temple and offer the customary sacrifices to God.[9]

Pompey arrived to help end the Hasmonean civil war but did not stay for long. Rome organized their empire into a system of client states meant to ensure a balance of power and the preservation of Roman interests without direct Roman occupation. Palestine became a province of Rome but was not ruled by force at this point.

Pompey appointed one of the Hasmonean brothers, Hyrcanus, to be king, though he had little power. The adviser to this king was **Antipater,** an Idumean, a people hated by the Jews. He quickly ingratiated himself with Rome and was made a Roman citizen, a right that would be passed on to his children. Antipater consolidated his power by helping Rome in their struggle against the Parthians. His sons were appointed governors to help rule. **Herod** was made governor in Galilee, and Phasael in Jerusalem. Herod came to be admired by both the Galilean Jews and Roman officials. When his father was poisoned by one of his rivals, Herod stepped into his father's former position as adviser to the ineffective Hasmonean king, Hyrcanus.

---

9. S. Kent Brown and Richard Holzapfel, *Between the Testaments: From Malachi to Matthew*, 82–83.

Herod the Great

Herod, an Idumean (Edom), was a third-generation Jew born into an aristocratic family in the late 70s BC (usually dated at 73 BC). Two of his siblings, Joseph and Salome, had Jewish names—an indication of the family's close association with Judaism. Herod married Mariamne I, a Hasmonean princess.

> Although the marriage connected him with the powerful Hasmoneans, it also appears to be a marriage of love. Later, he would marry the daughter of a Jewish temple priest, thus tying himself to the leading priestly families of his kingdom. Members of the Herodian family intermarried in complex and multiple ways, spinning a web of threads to royal and aristocratic families in an attempt to cinch down political and economic stability in the region.[10]

When civil war threatened once again, brought on by the continually warring Hasmonean family, Herod made his way to Rome for help in 40 BC. He was completely surprised when the outcome was his nomination to become king of Judea by Mark Anthony.[11] As he came to power, Herod chose dependency on Rome as the best strategy for assuring the welfare of the nation and for sustaining Judaism. After two and a half decades of strife in the region, Herod sought to unify the people and establish tranquility. Under the Roman umbrella, Herod advanced his nation from being a small, landlocked state to one that rivaled the ancient Israelite kingdoms of David and Solomon.[12]

Herod's first act upon receiving his new appointment was to mount the steps of Jupiter's temple in Rome, and flanked by Mark Anthony and Octavian, he offered sacrifice to that god. This act would characterize his reign: He would continually walk a fine line between his regard for Rome and his loyalty to Judaism. This is reflected in one of his first acts upon entering Jerusalem: he showed respect for Jewish law by ending the Hasmonean practice of uniting the political and

---

10. S. Kent Brown and Richard Holzapfel, *Between the Testaments: From Malachi to Matthew*, 82–83.
11. Flavius Josephus, *Antiquities of the Jews*, 14.15.5.
12. S. Kent Brown and Richard Holzapfel, *Between the Testaments: From Malachi to Matthew*, 92.

religious authority in one person. He would not serve as high priest, but he *would* appoint the high priest.

Herod's own family was filled with intrigue, murder, and revenge. He had his beloved wife, Mariamne, killed for treason, as well as two of his sons. The Hasmonean family alliance brought him a great deal of trouble. Their feuds continued throughout his lifetime. He was haunted by the death of Mariamne until his own death in 4 BC. He had a total of ten wives and a convoluted family line, in which a granddaughter married his grandson, and a niece, her uncle.

Herod is known for his extensive building enterprises, including the engineering marvel of the harbor at Caesarea and the beautification and enlargement of the temple. He helped finance the Olympic Games and was appointed president of the games, a post without precedent. Herod did much to protect Jews outside of Judea. With his help and influence, Jews of the Diaspora were guaranteed freedom to worship, to follow their dietary and sabbatical laws, to send the temple tax to Jerusalem as prescribed in the Mosaic law, and to avoid military service in the Roman army. Herod may have even helped finance a synagogue in the imperial capital itself since the Jews there named a synagogue in his honor. Herod brought his nation into an unprecedented era of productivity and prosperity.

The book written by Brown and Holzapfel, *Between the Testaments*, portrays a different picture of Herod than what we normally see. They emphasize his loyalty to Judaism, his generosity to his people, his emphasis on caring for the elderly and the infirm, and his fairness.

There is no question, however, that Herod felt a love and loyalty for Rome as well. While he did build the temple, he also had a Roman eagle mounted over one of the temple gates, an abomination to the Jews. He encouraged Greek and Roman learning, including the gymnasium. He contributed to the building of Roman temples for their gods and idols.

Herod did maintain a degree of popularity with the people, particularly among the Sadducees, who were mostly from the upper classes. Rome was well pleased with Herod's ability to keep the troublesome province of Palestine under control. However, following Herod's death, the Romans divided the kingdom among Herod's three sons, all to some degree ineffective. Philip ruled north and east of Galilee, Herod Antipas ruled Galilee and Perea, and Archelaus ruled Judea, Samaria, and Idumea. Because of his extreme and oppressive measures, the Jews were successful in having Archelaus removed in AD 6. His territory was then given to Herod Antipas to rule.

The Priests and the Priesthood

> From the days of the decree of King Cyrus of Persia (538 BC), priests and Levites stood at the top of the governing structure of life in the land of Judah. This situation arose because the Jerusalem temple and its altar formed the center of people's lives.[13]

When the first refugees from Babylon returned to Jerusalem to rebuild the temple, all priests had to produce their genealogical qualifications to serve in the temple or the privilege was denied them.[14] Jeshua, descended from the high priest Zadok, officiated in the temple ordinances.[15] Zadok had been the high priest who officiated in the dedication of Solomon's temple and, in vision, Ezekiel foresaw the control of the latter-day Jerusalem temple entrusted to the sons of Zadok.[16] Jeshua's presence was seen as an important sign to the people, and the descendants of the Zadok family did, in fact, control the temple until about 200 BC.

When Malachi prophesied (460s to 450s BC), he chastised the priests for their carelessness and lack of reverence. Furthermore, their offerings were polluted and flawed.[17] The people were marrying outside of the covenant, not paying tithing, divorcing, and not valuing the covenant family.[18]

---

13. S. Kent Brown and Richard Holzapfel, *Between the Testaments: From Malachi to Matthew*, 159.
14. Ezra 2:62.
15. Ezra 3:8.
16. Ezekiel 40:46; 43:19; 44:15.
17. Malachi 1:7–8, 10–14.
18. Malachi 2:8, 11, 14–15; 3:8–11.

When Ezra the scribe/priest arrived in Jerusalem (428 BC), he found that priests and Levites (among others) had married "strange wives" outside of the covenant. Ezra read the Law to all of the people of Jerusalem and encouraged the priests to take an oath to divorce themselves from their non-covenantal wives in order to continue in their duties.[19] This they did after a period of repentance and mourning.

The priestly family of Zadok had controlled the temple as high priests until the reign of the Seleucid king Antiochus IV. He appointed a priest named Jason as the high priest in exchange for a large sum of money. "*Not until this moment in Jewish history was the high priest appointed by an occupying power.*"[20]

Three years after Jason was appointed, a man named Menelaus, who was not a member of the high priestly family, offered more money than Jason did to King Antiochus and received the job. Menelaus began to take items from the temple to pay the bribe he had promised to the king. When Antiochus plundered the temple in 169 BC, Menelaus helped the king steal articles from the temple, including gold leafing.[21]

Following the success of the Maccabean/Hasmonean family in retaking Jerusalem and the cleansing and rededication of the temple, major changes took place in the high priesthood. After the deaths of Antiochus IV and Judas Maccabeus, Judas's brother Jonathan was chosen by the people to be their commander in the continuing war against the Seleucids. When the new Seleucid king came to the throne, he appointed this same Jonathan as the new high priest in Jerusalem. In 152 BC during the Feast of Tabernacles, Jonathan officiated as the high priest for the first time, beginning a 115-year role for his family. They were the first high priests who were *not* descendants of Zadok.

For an unknown reason, pilgrims attending the Feast of Tabernacles in Jerusalem threw citrons at Alexander Jannaeus (103–76 BC) while he officiated in the office of high priest. His forces swiftly and brutally gained control, slaughtering around six thousand rioters. The

---

19. Ezra 10:1–5, 18–24.
20. S. Kent Brown and Richard Holzapfel, *Between the Testaments: From Malachi to Matthew*, 49–51.
21. Ibid.

Hasmonean/Maccabean line continued to degenerate, but even after Rome took control of Palestine, one of the Hasmonean line was appointed as high priest.

When Herod came to power, he ended the Hasmonean practice of uniting the role of king and priest. However, he did continue the practice of appointing the high priest himself. He appointed a succession of high priests and deposed them at will. Some were murdered. A new pattern emerged: "The chief Roman official in Jerusalem would hand the office of high priest to a person who belonged to one of a few prominent families of priests."[22] A position that formerly was a lifelong call now was held as long as one pleased the local ruler. The family that produced Annas and his son-in-law Caiaphas, known from the New Testament gospels, would see no fewer than eight high priests, none apparently serving until his death.

> To make matters even worse, during the years of Herod's reign and beyond, he and his successors in governmental office kept custody of the high priest's ceremonial robes. Each time the high priest needed to dress in his robes for an important holiday, he had to go to the ruler and ask for them. By this device, Herod and the others kept the high priest and his associates under their control.[23]

Temple worship lapsed into mere ritual, and the spiritual breath of Israel nearly ceased. Some life, however, did remain. Some of the seed of Levi continued to honor the priesthood (as seen in the priest Zacharias).[24]

The Scribes

> As long as Israel had prophets, the scribes remained teachers and copyists. But when the prophetic voice ceased in Israel, these experts in the Law of Moses began to fill the vacuum.[25]

Ezra, sent by King Artaxerxes (428 BC) to appoint magistrates and judges and to teach the Law of God unto all that did not know

22. S. Kent Brown and Richard Holzapfel, *Between the Testaments: From Malachi to Matthew*, 168.
23. Ibid., 170.
24. See "Between the Testaments," *Old Testament Student Manual.*
25. Ibid.

it, was a righteous scribe/priest who had a tremendous impact upon the people of Jerusalem. He is the first scribe that we see mentioned in the scriptures and is held in reverence and respect and almost seen as a prophet, although he does not seem to have claimed revelation. He introduced religious reforms that would outlast him by hundreds of years based upon the written law.

The scriptures had been written in Hebrew, but the language of the people shifted to that of the population where they resided. Therefore, the scribes became interpreters of the scriptures, reading and explaining them to the people in their own tongue. "It should not be surprising that there was no unity of interpretation among these scholars, nor that they worked to bring men to their particular point of view."[26]

> During the Intertestamental period, a feeling began to blossom that almost any person could study and come to understand the Law. In the era before the fall of Jerusalem, teaching the Law had been the responsibility of the priests and Levites.[27] Now a cadre of scribes rose up—men who wanted to understand and teach the Law. These scribes became the guardians of the Law and influenced how common folk came to regard its precepts.[28]

Other titles used for scribes: lawyers, doctors, elders, and rabbis.

The Pharisees

Although there is disagreement as to origin and date of this group, many agree that both the Pharisees and Sadducees gained prominence when Judah was trying to cope with the strong Hellenizing efforts of the Seleucids. "The roots of all Jewish sects go back into the era of the Babylonian captivity, but by the time the Maccabean/Hasmonean revolt was over, both parties had become powerful and rival sects."[29]

---

26. Ibid.
27. Deuteronomy 33:10.
28. S. Kent Brown and Richard Holzapfel, *Between the Testaments: From Malachi to Matthew*, 145, 172.
29. "Between the Testaments," *Old Testament Student Manual.*

The Pharisees probably evolved from a group called the *Hasidim*, a name meaning "the holy ones."[30] Brown and Holzapfel call the group the *Hasideans*, meaning "loving kindness." They state that the *Hasideans* were driven into the Maccabean camp after a savage attack upon their members during a Sabbath, led by the Seleucids. Although they maintained their soldierly support for the Hasmonean family, "The Hasideans were the first among the sons of Israel to seek peace."[31] Their efforts were unappreciated. The newly appointed Hellenized high priest Alcimus, in conjunction with the Seleucid governor, had sixty of the Hasideans executed, creating an even deeper distrust and hatred of any form of Greek culture.[32]

While the *Old Testament Manual* and several others state that the Pharisees originated from the *Hasidim* or *Hasideans*, Brown and Holzapfel make the point that a direct link to the *Hasidim* or *Hasideans* cannot be proven, and they believe that they were a separate group.[33]

The Pharisees promoted the observance of Jewish rituals and the study of the Torah. Some took a vow to separate themselves from the impurities of those living around them and to follow strictly their interpretation of the Law. Not only did they honor the written scriptures, but they also enlarged upon them, trying to adapt old codes to new conditions, leading to the institution of an oral law, which was held in as high esteem as the written law. To counteract the Greek influences, they turned to a strict, almost rigid, obedience to the Law.

> Because of their attempts to keep themselves separate from the worldly taint of false ideas, this group began to be called the *powrashim*, from the Hebrew *powrash*, which means "to be separated." Thus evolved the name *Pharisees*, which is the Greek transliteration of *powrashim*.[34]

---

30. Ibid.
31. 1 Maccabees 7:14; see bible.usccb.org.
32. S. Kent Brown and Richard Holzapfel, *Between the Testaments: From Malachi to Matthew*, 175–76.
33. Ibid., 177–78
34. "Between the Testaments," *Old Testament Student Manual.*

> Another possibility is that the word Pharisee derives from the Hebrew verb "to expound" and points to them as expounders of the Law of Moses.[35]
>
> They believed that Moses received two laws on Mount Sinai, one that he wrote down and one that he passed on orally. It is this latter, the source of "the tradition of the elders," that Jesus and His disciples objected to.[36] For Pharisees, this oral tradition was the real governing influence in how a person was to understand the Law; and, in the view of the Pharisees, they had received the oral law from Moses himself. (See *Mishnah* Pirke Aboth 1:1.)[37]

Ironically, their zeal toward the Law became "another form of idolatry, because their worship was of the Law instead of the Lawgiver."[38]

Because they had given their support to the Maccabean revolt and the Hasmonean family, the Pharisees appealed to the majority of the population and constituted a much larger group than the Sadducees. There were few Pharisees who rose to positions of power either under the Hasmonean priest-kings or under Herod and his Roman successors. They did seek to make changes, acting as a political-action group. From what we can learn, they were neither reclusive nor outlandish in their public behavior. Unlike the priests, Sadducees, and Zealots, the Pharisees remained a force within the society beyond the fall of Jerusalem and its temple in AD 70. The Pharisees continued on as the rabbis of later ages, and the Judaism of late antiquity was the child of Pharisaic teachings and ideals.

The Pharisees believed in a combination of free will and predestination, in the resurrection of the dead, and in a judgment resulting in reward or punishment in the life to come.[39] They also believed that angels and spirits inhabit the heavens.

---

35. Ibid.
36. Matthew 15:2; Mark 7:3.
37. "Between the Testaments," *Old Testament Student Manual.*
38. Ibid.
39. *Encyclopedia Judaica*, "Pharisees."

The Sadducees

The Sadducees were comprised mostly from the upper level of society—priests, merchants, and aristocrats. It was among this wealthy class that the Greek culture was being embraced; thus, the Sadducees were not popular with the majority of the people. The name of the sect (*Zedukim* in Hebrew) is probably derived from Zadok, the high priest in the days of King Solomon. "Hence, the name *Sadducees* referred to those who were sympathetic with the Zadokites."[40] The family of Zadok controlled the temple functions until about 200 BC.

Unlike the Pharisees, the Sadducees rejected the oral law, but they went even further in accepting only the Pentateuch—the first five books of Moses as scripture. They seem not to have accepted the historical and prophetic books as canonical. They did not believe in an afterlife, and therefore did not believe in a resurrection. They did not believe in angels or divine spirits in heaven. They believed the purpose for keeping the Law was for divine assistance in mortality. No symbolic or allegorical interpretation, a favorite of the Pharisees, was allowed.

By the time of Jesus, the Sadducees, although not popular among the common people, controlled the Sanhedrin and the office of the high priest. But with the fall of Jerusalem and the temple to the Romans in AD 70, the Sadducees disappeared. The majority of them were priests, and their chief reason for existence disappeared with the loss of the temple.

The Zealots

The Zealots were radical extremists who opposed Rome and the Hellenization of Judah. They pledged themselves to be agents of divine wrath and judgment against idolatry, apostasy, and transgression of the Law. They accepted the theology of redemption through zeal for the Law and sought to bring in the kingdom of God by a violent struggle against Roman overlords. Many believe that they are

---

40. Ibid., "Sadducees."

responsible for bringing the Roman retribution that resulted in the destruction of Jerusalem and the temple in AD 70. Their hatred was equally distributed between the Roman government and the Jewish society elite who embraced Hellenization. They believed that only God was their master and refused to call any person "master."

The Zealots were "zealous for God" and gave justification for their actions on a model from the scriptures. Phinehas, the grandson of Aaron, was commended by the Lord because "he was zealous for my sake" when he slew an Israelite man and a Midianite woman whilst they were "consorting" in the man's tent. A plague had descended upon the Israelites because of their licentiousness with the daughters of Moab and Midian. Not only had they been consorting with non-covenantal women, but they had also been bowing down to their false gods. Phinehas's action stopped the plague that had already killed 24,000 people. As a reward, the Lord covenanted to give him an everlasting priesthood "because he was zealous for his God, and made an atonement for the children of Israel."[41]

"Simon called Zelotes" was Jesus's eleventh Apostle and most likely a Zealot. There is also a hint from Josephus that Barabbas, who was released at the time of Christ's crucifixion, was likely a Zealot.[42] The Zealot movement died with the burning of the temple in AD 70, but for one branch of the movement, the *sicarii*, the end came at Masada.

> The *sicarii* were assassins. They carried a distinctive knife that they folded into their robes that is called in Latin *sica*, meaning "dagger." They targeted not only Roman officials but also Jewish notables who seemed to foster the status quo or, worse, to side with the Romans.[43]

The Essenes

The Essene origins began when the crisis with Hellenism occurred and precipitated the Maccabean War. Their name has been traced to two root words, one meaning "pious," and another meaning "healers."

---

41. Numbers 25:1–13.
42. S. Kent Brown and Richard Holzapfel, *Between the Testaments: From Malachi to Matthew*, 205.
43. Ibid.

Their founder was known only as the "Teacher of Righteousness" and was a priest. While they allied themselves at first with the Maccabean/Hasmoneans, they were later critical and dismayed with the corruption of the Hasmonean family, ultimately rejecting their right to the high priesthood and their authority at the temple, feeling that the temple services were polluted.

They withdrew from society to the shores of the Dead Sea, adopting a path of an intensely personal approach to spirituality. Some re-entered society for a time during the reign of Herod, approving of His reforms to government and support of the Jewish laws. Herod also held the Essenes in high esteem because of a prophecy by one of them that he would become king.[44]

In their withdrawal from society, they established a community at Qumran and waited for the Messiah and His prophet who would precede Him. They believed that two messiahs would come—one from the house of Aaron and one from the house of David. They also looked for a prophet who would precede the messiahs based on Moses's prophecy about a "prophet from among their brethren."[45]

The Essene life was not easy.

> Leaders issued three items to potential members: a white robe, a white apron or girdle, and a trowel with which to take care of latrine needs. With these items, potential members began a one-year trial period. At the end of one year, leaders of the group reviewed each initiate's performance and decided whether to let the person continue into a second trial period of two more years. If the person was allowed to continue, he received permission to participate in the ritual of the daily bath. If all worked well thereafter, that person was admitted into full membership at the end of the three years and could eat the common meals with the group. The oaths that a new member swore about eating only foods prepared within the community meant that a person who left the Essene fellowship would literally starve to death. Before the midday meal, members bathed.

44. S. Kent Brown and Richard Holzapfel, *Between the Testaments: From Malachi to Matthew*, 98, 201.
45. Deuteronomy 18:18.

> Membership also involved a strict observance of the Sabbath day, not taking care of any personal needs on that day. In addition, each individual gave up all property to the group, including daily earnings.[46]

Essenes did look for a day when the temple would be cleansed and purified by the Lord. It still played a major, though future, role in their practice and belief. They believed in a hierarchical system of angels who inhabit the heavens and whose names they were not to reveal, treating them as sacred and secret. They believed in a predestined world. They did not believe in a resurrection and thought that a person's soul inherits a bodiless eternity. They thought of the body as a tomb. They were also anti-Ephraimite, and in their writings referred to Ephraim and Manasseh as wicked liars and apostates "who seek smooth things during the last days."[47]

The Samaritans

The Samaritans have been discussed to some extent in the previous chapter.

When the Jews returned from Babylon to build the temple, the Samaritans were quick to offer help, but the Jews refused them, considering them to be unclean and corrupt. This cemented the old enmity, and the Samaritans hampered and hindered the building of the temple and the city walls.[48] Shortly thereafter, the Samaritans built their own temple to Jehovah on Mount Gerizim.[49]

Although the Samaritans viewed themselves as fully Israelite and venerated Moses, they seemed to easily embrace the Greek culture, and under pressure of the Seleucid rule of Antiochus IV, they converted their temple to the worship of Zeus. John Hyrcanus, a member of the Maccabean/Hasmonean family, led forces against the Samaritan city

---

46. S. Kent Brown and Richard Holzapfel, *Between the Testaments: From Malachi to Matthew*, 198–99.
47. Ibid, 200.
48. Ezra 4:1–4.
49. Deuteronomy 11:29; John 4:20.

of Shechem and destroyed the Samaritan temple on Mount Gerizim in 128 BC, thus magnifying the enmity between the Samaritans and the Jews.

The Jews looked upon the Samaritans with such enmity that they would take a lengthy detour around Samaria when traveling from Galilee to Judea rather than to face contamination.

CHRONOLOGY of the JEWS

Date	Event	Impact on Jewish People
587 BC	Destruction of Jerusalem by Babylon. Temple burnt, city walls broken.	Many carried as captives into Babylonian Empire. Allowed to maintain their worship. Many prospered in trade and so forth.
538 BC	Median/Persian Empire conquers Babylon under leadership of King Cyrus.	Cyrus is the first known king to issue a proclamation on human rights. He is welcomed by the people whose empires he conquered.
537 BC	Cyrus decrees that the Jews may return to Jerusalem and rebuild the temple. He sends financial aid and the temple treasures that had been confiscated by Nebuchadnezzar. This is direct fulfillment of prophecy made by Isaiah, wherein the Lord called Cyrus His "shepherd" who would rebuild the temple (Isa. 44:28).	Very few Jews respond to the opportunity. It is some time before a group goes to Jerusalem to begin building the temple.
536 BC?	Zerubbabel leads a group of Jews to Jerusalem to begin building the temple. This is a small group who struggle greatly with poverty and conditions in Jerusalem.	Jews continue to prosper in the Persian Empire; show little interest in returning to Jerusalem. Those who do go to Jerusalem are quickly discouraged. Temple work halts or goes very slowly.

Date	Event	Impact on Jewish People
522 BC	Darius I becomes king of the Persian Empire. Daniel in lion's den (Dan. 6). Darius commands, "I make a decree, that in every dominion of my kingdom men tremble and fear before the God of Daniel: for he is the living God" (Dan. 6:26).	
520 BC	Daniel fasts and prays for Jerusalem (Dan. 9:1–3).	
520–519 BC	Haggai and Zechariah prophesy in Jerusalem, encouraging the building of the temple to proceed.	Energy and hope seem to be renewed. The work on the temple goes forward. Not more than 20,000 live in Jerusalem at this time.
515 BC	Temple completed.	The people rejoice—and weep; the temple is a pale shadow of the temple of Solomon.
486 BC	Queen Esther—Ahasuerus (Xerxes).	Esther saved the Jewish people from annihilation throughout the Persian Empire. For Esther to hide her Jewish identity from her husband implies that the Jewish people were still seen as an inferior race.
460s–450s BC	Malachi prophesies.	The last prophet to speak "in the name of the Lord." Priests lazy, careless, not offering pure sacrifices. People divorcing, not paying tithing, not keeping covenant.

Date	Event	Impact on Jewish People
445 BC	Nehemiah, cup bearer to King Artaxerxes, pleads with the King to be sent to help build Jerusalem. Artaxerxes appoints him governor of Jerusalem and sends treasury funds to help in the project. Nehemiah leads the people of Jerusalem in rebuilding the walls of Jerusalem.	With the building of the walls of Jerusalem and Nehemiah's leadership as governor, a sense of nationalistic feeling returns.
428 BC	Ezra the scribe/priest leaves Persia with the blessings and further monetary assistance of King Artaxerxes. The King instructs him to appoint magistrates and judges and to teach the law of the Lord to those that did not know it (Ezra 7:25). Ezra worked in conjunction with Nehemiah to restore Judah to its former strength. Ezra read and interpreted the law to the people in Jerusalem. He also instructed them to divorce themselves from the wives they had married outside of the covenant and to purify themselves to be worthy vessels of the Lord.	The people of Jerusalem "sat in the street of the house of God, trembling because of this matter, and for the great rain" (Ezra 10:9). Repentance and spiritual cleansing took place, as well as rededication to the law of God.
332 BC	Alexander the Great conquered Jerusalem.	"Hellenization" (to make all things Greek), the greatest challenge yet to face the people of Israel, begins to take hold of the known world.
301 BC	Ptolemies take control of Judea.	Allow relative autonomy.

Date	Event	Impact on Jewish People
200 BC	Seleucids capture and control Judea.	Much more aggressive in the manner in which they rule.
175 BC	Antiochus IV comes to power.	Tremendous pressure upon the people to conform to Greek ideals and principles.
169 BC	Antiochus IV plunders and desecrates the temple. Sabbath observance, celebrations, and circumcision forbidden on penalty of death. Pigs, unclean under the Mosaic law, offered as sacrifice in the temple. People forced to worship Zeus and other gods. Antiochus appoints the high priest, the first time the high priest is chosen by the local ruler.	Thousands die for maintaining their religion. Some comply, but most wait for a chance to overthrow this government.
167 BC	Mattathias, a priest from the Asmonean (Hasmonean) family, refuses to offer sacrifice to a pagan god. He slays his fellow priest who begins to comply, along with the Syrian soldier who gave the order. He and his five sons flee to the hills and call for all of Judah to join with them.	Rebellion!
164 BC	Under the leadership of Mattathias's son, Judah the Maccabee or Judas Maccabeas, Jerusalem is retaken and the temple cleansed. The miracle of Hanukkah.	People see the Maccabean family as great deliverers and give them high honors.

Date	Event	Impact on Jewish People
164 BC	Judas Maccabeas makes an alliance with Rome, seeking help in overthrowing the Seleucids.	No real leadership from Rome until 63 BC.
152 BC	Jonathan, Judas's brother, is appointed high priest, beginning a 115-year role for the Hasmonean family.	Priesthood not belonging to the line of Zadok. The high priest is appointed by the local ruler.
142 BC	Under the leadership of the Hasmonean/Maccabean family, Palestine becomes independent for the first time in 440 years.	The Hasmoneans quickly become corrupt, their own in-fighting causes civil war, and two of the Hasmonean brothers ask Rome for help, effectively ending Judah's independence.
63 BC	Pompey takes Judea for Rome.	Judah becomes a "client state." Hyrcanus II (Hasmonean) is appointed "king" with Antipas (Herod's father) as his counselor.
40 BC	Herod "the Great" made king of Judea.	Great prosperity, numerous building projects, beautification and enlargement of the temple. Relative peace under "Pax Romana."

Dates approximate and based on the Bible Dictionary's "Chronology"; *Between the Testaments—From Malachi to Matthew*, by Brown and Holzapfel; and the *Old Testament Student Manual* of The Church of Jesus Christ of Latter-day Saints.

CHAPTER 20

Judah in Agony

AD 70

The Roman destruction of Jerusalem and the temple in AD 70 was in response to a Jewish revolt that was instigated by the zealots. Although the citizens in Jerusalem were divided politically, the zealots sought to force them to unite in fighting their Roman overlords by burning the food stores that had been preserved in the city. The zealots killed any of the leading citizens who sought peace with Rome. By burning the food stores, the zealots thought they would unite the Jews in a desperate fight against extinction. They were doomed to fail.

Rome sent additional troops to quell the rebellion, resulting in a terrible slaughter of the Jewish people and another captivity for Judah. The historian Josephus, who lived at the time, claimed that over one million Jewish people were killed and that 97,000 were taken away in slavery.[1]

Persecution Solidifies Jewish Faithfulness

Suspicion and hatred toward this unique group of people who would not assimilate or syncretize with the culture and religion of the people among whom they were transported has resulted in tremendous anguish for the Jewish people. The more pressure that was put

1. Flavius Josephus, *Wars of the Jews*, 6:9:3.

upon them to comply to the standards of the current trends of society, the more they bonded themselves to their unique identity as a group and the more they resisted and set themselves apart through their own adherence to the Law of Moses as they understood it. They kept to their dietary laws, wore their religious clothing, and adhered to following one God, even while living in communities that worshipped a pantheon of deities.

Christian Persecution of the Tribe of Judah

The relentless persecution of the Jews has resulted in their agony throughout the centuries. Horrifyingly, since the fourth century, when Christianity became the official religion of the Roman Empire, most of that persecution has been performed by Christians and in the name of Christ. Determined to punish the whole of Judah for a handful of priests and elite leaders who decided Jesus should die, Christians have threatened, terrified, and murdered countless innocent Jewish people.

To be clear, Jesus was a Jew. His apostles were Jews, and the first converts to the Church were Jewish.

The priests, Annas and Caiaphas, who had determined that Jesus should die,[2] should have been from the tribe of Levi in accordance with the Law of Moses, and therefore not technically Jewish.

We don't know how many people stood in Pilate's courtyard demanding Jesus's blood.[3] It was in the early morning hours that the priests and their emissaries took Jesus to Pilate.[4] They had held their illegal trial of Jesus during the midnight hours, after the men had performed their ritual "Night of Watchings" with the Passover where they were to stay awake and watch for the Messiah.[5] And with that Passover, there was so much to do for priest and populace: the priests would be required to start early with the morning sacrifices at the temple beginning at 9:00 a.m. The men of the general populace, weary from staying awake the night before, may be sleeping, their wives

2. John 11:49–51; 18:31–31; Luke 23:10; Mark 15:1; Matthew 26:3–4, 63–66; 27:1.
3. Matthew 27:25.
4. John 18:28.
5. Lynda Cherry, *The Feasts and Festivals of the Messiah.*

either cleaning up from the Passover meal held the previous night or gathering supplies to celebrate the Passover that night. (Passover would have been counted as sundown to sundown, Jesus and His apostles "keeping" Passover on the first night, whereas the priests and wealthier citizens celebrated the second.)[6] It would seem impossible for the whole of Jewry to stop their preparations and chores to go and demand Jesus's death from Pilate. And even so, did not Jesus Himself testify that He must die?[7] His atoning sacrifice was necessary in order to fulfill the Plan of Salvation.

Nevertheless, many Christians have justified their persecution of the Jews by blaming the entire race for Jesus's death. Malcolm Hay shares the following about Jewish persecution during the Middle Ages:

> The most trivial pretext was often enough to start a massacre. In 1011, a slight earthquake, accompanied by a high wind, disturbed at Rome the celebration of Easter. The Jews were accused of having produced both the earthquake and the storm by means of their magical practices. After some of them had been put to the sword, "the fury of the wind was appeased."[8]

Persecution During the Crusades

The first Crusades (1096, 1147) to "free Jerusalem" were celebrated by first "expelling the infidel" out of the Christian countries where they lived. For many in Europe, this meant first turning on the Jews, forcing them to either accept baptism into the Christian church, or death. Many Jews chose suicide. Some had their children stolen from them to be baptized and raised as Christians by their neighbors. Those who had been forcibly baptized were expected to live according to the rule of the Church and were watched closely for any prevarication for which they would be made to suffer. With the Second Crusade, Pope Innocent III determined that in order to expiate their sins against

---

6. Ibid.
7. Matthew 16:21; 17:22–23; Mark 8:31.
8. Malcolm Hay, *Europe and the Jews*, 37.

Jesus, the Jews should be forced to pay for the Crusade and added that any debts that crusaders owed to Jews would be absolved.[9]

Under the guise of protecting them, emperors Henry IV and Conrad III responded to the persecution of the Jews during the first two Crusades by making the Jews "serfs [servants] of the royal chamber." While supposedly under the protection of the emperors, in reality they became the *property* of the royals and were bought, sold, and loaned from one household to another. Edward H. Flannery notes that "Kings paid off barons and barons paid off creditors with Jews." Kings would, for a consideration, transfer to nobles or townships the right to posses "his" Jews.[10] The practice spread from Germany to France and England.

Perpetual Servitude

Pope Innocent III (1198–1216) "spoke of the 'perpetual servitude' of the Jews, and the Third Lateran Council (1179) of the 'subjection' of Jews to Christians." Even St. Thomas Aquinas acknowledged the rightness of Jewish servitude to Church and State, and English Jurist Bracton wrote, "The Jew cannot have anything of his own. Whatever he acquires he acquires not for himself but for the king."[11]

In 1215, the Fourth Lateran Council decreed that all Jews (and Saracens) were to wear a badge that would mark them for their race so that Christians would not mingle or intermarry with them.

In order to keep suspicion and hatred alive so that they could use the Jews as they would, malicious stories were spread that certain Jewish groups had kidnapped a Christian boy here or there, had crucified him, drained him of his blood, and used his blood for the Paschal/Passover celebrations. One such story involved a twelve-year-old boy, William, who was found murdered in Norwich. His death was unexplained, and there was no evidence whatsoever to link him to the Jews, but a monk, Thomas of Monmouth, claimed that William had been tortured and killed by the Jews. Despite the lack of evidence

9. Edward Flannery, *The Anguish of the Jews*, 91–96; Malcolm Hay, *Europe and the Jews*, 41–73.
10. Edward Flannery, *The Anguish of the Jews*, 95.
11. Ibid., 96.

to back up any such accusation, rumors spread quickly throughout Europe, each country claiming to have their own little Christian saint for whom they were massacring Jews.[12]

In addition, the Jews, who were forced to be servants or subjects of the king and were not allowed to claim anything for themselves, were virtually forced by those same rulers into money lending, for which they were accused of usury (collecting interest) and persecuted.[13]

In fact, the first Jews to arrive in England were brought by William the Conqueror in 1066 so that they would provide funding for his conquests. The Jews lived in relative peace there until jealousy arose along with accusations that they were making money from the very business they had been forced to employ. They were taxed heavily, so the interest they earned from their businesses typically benefited the crown directly.

> By the late 1200s, a series of laws had been created restricting the rights of the Jewish people. For instance, they were not allowed to own land, and after their death, their money went, not to their children, but directly to the Crown. In 1275 King Edward I passed a law forbidding the Jews from usury. They were entitled to earn a living as tradesmen or farmers but were not allowed to be part of guilds or to own farmland. The Jews became poor, and the king could no longer collect taxes from them. Many hundreds were arrested, hanged, or imprisoned. And then finally in 1290, they were banished from England altogether. Jews were not allowed to return to England until 1656.[14]

Expulsion and Banishment

France followed England's example and expelled or banished the Jews in 1306 after numerous threats that the expulsion was coming. Many of the refugees made their way to Spain and Germany, where a number of Jews had lived for centuries, but they were not safe in either country.

---

12. Malcolm Hay, *Europe and the Jews*, 111–39.
13. Edward Flannery, *The Anguish of the Jews*, 96–98.
14. British Library, "Expulsion of Jews from England."

Despite the questionable results of the Spanish Inquisition, where Jews were tortured into converting to Christianity or died, Grand Inquisitor Tomas de Torquemada still did not trust the Jews and urged Queen Isabella and King Ferdinand to expel all Jews from Spain entirely. In 1492, Isabella and Ferdinand issued the Alhambra Decree, mandating that all Jews be expelled from Spain.

> Estimation is difficult, but modern historians now believe around 40,000 Jews emigrated, with older estimates putting the number at several hundred thousand. Many died trying to reach safety, and in some cases it is believed that refugees paid for passage to other countries only to be thrown overboard by Spanish captains. While the Ottoman Empire welcomed the influx of Spanish Jews, many other nations in Europe treated them as cruelly as the Spaniards—though Portugal was a popular destination, its rulers issued a similar decree five years later.[15]

Spain formally revoked the Alhambra Decree in 1968.

Blamed for the Black Death

When the Black Death attacked Europe, accusations arose that the Jews were poisoning the waters and bringing the Death upon Christians, even though Jewish families were also suffering and dying under the plague.

In 1348, Germany led Europe in blaming Jews for the Black Death and persecuting them for it. Pope Clement VI tried to stop the torture of the Jews and issued the Papal bull *Sicut Judaeis*, stating that the church would protect the Jews and calling on Christians to stop killing them. However, the German Emperor Charles IV did not openly support the Pope's decree and turned a blind eye to the persecution. Many Jews were tortured in order to force a confession that they had, indeed, poisoned the waters. In the town of Basel, all of the Jews were brought to a house built for the purpose and burned alive. Hundreds of other German towns followed suit, burning their Jewish neighbors and baptizing their children. In Strasburg, it took six days for the townspeople to finish annihilating the Jews, first robbing and

15. "Spain Announces It Will Expel All Jews," history.com.

stripping them naked and then herding them to be burned alive. The slaughter began on the set date of February 14, St. Valentine's Day.[16]

> Persecutions took place on dates commemorating St. Nicholas; the Conception of Mary, the Holy Virgin; the feast of St. John, the Apostle; St. Bartholomew's day; the feast of St. Matthew; and the feast of the Circumcision of the Lord. Also, many cities murdered their Jews in association with Lent including the first Sunday associated with that commemoration and the night of Shrove Tuesday. In addition, many communities killed their Jews on Sundays or Friday evenings. The persecution of Jews on Fridays may have taken place for two reasons. Clearly, this was the day on which Jesus was executed, but also, Friday evening was the beginning of the Jewish Sabbath. Clearly the executions which took place on Saturday also corresponded with the Jewish holy day.[17]

The Jews in Poland and Russia

The Jews were being pushed from country to country and desperately in need of a homeland. Many of them sought for safety and refuge in Poland. It's estimated that by the sixteenth century, eighty percent of all Jews worldwide lived in Poland and enjoyed relative tolerance and freedom. This freedom and tolerance was put into jeopardy when Russia took control of many areas of Poland and imposed a number of restrictions on Jewish life, confining Jews to the Pale of Settlement.[18]

Following the assassination of Russian Tsar Alexander II (1881), the Russian-Polish Jews became victims of "organized massacres targeting communities called pogroms."

> In response, some two million Jews emigrated out of this region, with the vast majority going to the United States. Others responded with different solutions. Some Orthodox Jews, who looked to protect Judaism, tried their best to isolate themselves from hostility and outside forces. Zionists promoted the idea of mass migration

---

16. Albert Winkler, "The Medieval Holocaust: The Approach of the Plague and the Destruction of Jews in Germany, 1348–49."
17. Ibid., 24.
18. Facing History and Ourselves, "Jewish Life in Poland before the Holocaust."

> to Palestine, while socialist Bundists sought to unite all the Jews in Eastern Europe in a class-based fight for economic reform. Others believed that assimilation (or acculturation) into mainstream culture was the proper response.[19]

After World War I, a series of pogroms and discriminatory laws were enforced against the Jews, and they had fewer opportunities to leave the country and emigrate. World War II was on the horizon, and Poland had the largest population of Jews of any European country, about three and a half million, or ten percent of the population.[20]

Even greater agony was yet to come.

The Holocaust

It is truly inconceivable that so many would follow the insane will of one man, Adolf Hitler, and consent to the torture and murder of millions of people simply because of their race.

When Hitler came to power, there were more Jews living in Germany than any other country in Western Europe.[21]

The United States Holocaust Memorial Museum states that

> The Holocaust was the systematic, state-sponsored persecution and murder of six million Jews by the Nazi regime and its collaborators between 1933 and 1945 across Europe and North Africa. The height of the persecution and murder occurred during World War II. By the end of the war in 1945, the Germans and their collaborators had killed nearly two out of every three European Jews.
>
> A new kind of antisemitism emerged in the second half of the 19th century. At its core was the theory that Jews were not merely a religious group but a separate "race." Antisemites believed Jews were dangerous and threatening because of their "Jewish blood." They believed that Jews would still be a threat even if a Jewish person converted to Christianity. Antisemitic racism united these new racial

---

19. Facing History and Ourselves, "Jewish Life in Poland Before the Holocaust."
20. Ibid.
21. Gerard Sloyan, "Christian Persecution of Jews over the Centuries."

theories with older anti-Jewish stereotypes. These ideas gained wide acceptance.[22]

Compassion and Respect for the Tribe of Judah

This chapter is not meant to be a full historical detail of the sufferings of the Jews. Many books have been written on the topic, and a few are listed in the footnotes. Frankly, I am not qualified to address the numerous atrocities perpetrated against the family of Judah or to speak in their behalf. For those who have been to the Yad Vashem memorial in Jerusalem, each flickering candle has its own story to tell, and each is reflected in a mirror of voices that reverberate and echo throughout the ages. The suffering they have endured is simply incomprehensible.

Many who are ignorant of the fact that the persecution of the Jews has been relentless throughout the centuries, ask me how it is possible that the Jewish people do not now recognize Jesus as their Messiah. I often feel to respond that so many horrors have been perpetrated against the Jews in the name of Christ that it would take a miraculous healing to pierce the wall of protection that has been placed around the Jewish heart.

It is the plight of the Jew and their response to that torment that provokes not only compassion in my own heart, but awe and great respect. As a collective, they have stood true to their ideals and to their understanding of what God requires of them. They have honored and preserved the sacred writings and teachings of the prophets. They have resisted assimilation into foreign empires and foreign beliefs, which for them includes Christianity. They have loved and cherished their families. They have borne and suffered much and deserve the compassion and regard of all humanity. Ultimately, they are God's people, and He has a covenant with them.

As recorded by the prophet Nephi in the Book of Mormon, God asks:

22. United States Holocaust Memorial Museum, "Frequently Asked Questions about the Holocaust for Educators."

> Do they [the Gentiles] remember the travails, and the labors, and the pains of the Jews, and their diligence unto me, in bringing salvation unto the Gentiles? O ye Gentiles, have ye remembered the Jews, mine ancient covenant people? Nay; but ye have cursed them, and have hated them, and have not sought to recover them. But behold, I will return all these things upon your own heads; for I the Lord have not forgotten my people.[23]

23. 2 Nephi 29:4–5

CHAPTER 21

To Joseph from Judah: Rabbi Israel's Letter to the Ten Tribes—1830

IN 1830, A GROUP OF RABBIS WHO EMIGRATED FROM EASTERN EUROPE to Jerusalem wrote a letter called "Epistle to the Ten Tribes." Led by Rabbi Israel ben Shmuel Ashkenazi of Shklov (1770–1839), the rabbis came to believe, based on a reading of the *Zohar,* that "a reunion between the lost ten tribes of Israel and the children of Judah was necessary before the Messiah would come and redeem His people."[1]

Rabbi Israel was the main author of the letter to the lost ten tribes. He had heard a rumor that someone had met a man who claimed to be from the tribe of Dan in Yemen. This greatly excited Rabbi Israel and many of his fellow scholars, who worked together in creating a formal plea for the ten tribes to "come home."[2]

The *Zohar* states: "For during the time of the Footsteps of the Messiah, some of our brethren of the Ten Tribes will be discovered."[3]

1. "Vilna Gaon's Students Letter to the Lost Tribes," sefaria.org.; "Letter to the Ten Lost Tribes of Israel," sefaria.org.
2. "Letter to the Ten Lost Tribes of Israel," sefaria.org.
3. Arie Morgenstern, "Attempt to Renew Rabbinic Ordination in Safed," *Hastening Redemption: Messianism and the Resettlement of the Land of Israel.*

Rabbi Israel believed that the ten tribes held certain keys to the redemption and restoration of Judah, the holy lands, and the temple. He wrote that there would be a certain order that would occur in that redemption and felt that anything taken out of order would corrupt the whole process. In other words, in his mind, Jerusalem would not be rebuilt until after the gathering and unification of the tribes began and proper judges, counselors, or those who were "ordained" by authority were called to lead them. He believed that the proper order would occur thusly:

- Ingathering of exiles
- Restoration of justice (or judges)
- Extirpation of apostates
- Reward for the righteous
- Rebuilding Jerusalem
- Messiah son of David to come
- Prayer of united Israel
- Renewal of temple service

Most interesting to the Latter-day Saint scholar would be Rabbi Israel's reliance on a teaching by Maimonides that the "renewal of ordination was a necessary precondition to the Messiah's advent" and that this ordination would "establish an authorized court of ordained sages" or judges.[4]

Maimonides taught that since the Jews did not have this proper ordination, the ten tribes must have a leader among them who possessed the ordination, or authority, and could thereby ordain others to sit in the councils of judges.[5] Arie Morgenstern explains that

> This was the first time in the history of Jewish messianism that there was an effort to assign the ten tribes a central role in the redemptive process through renewal of ordination. The ten tribes had always

4. "Vilna Gaon's Students Letter to the Lost Tribes," sefaria.org.; "Letter to the Ten Lost Tribes of Israel," sefaria.org.
5. Maimonides, *Sha'arei Zedeq le-Zera Yizhaq*, 40a.

been taken into account, particularly during times of messianic awakening, but only insofar as it was believed that they would be discovered at the end of days and might bring their military prowess to bear against the enemies of the Jews. Never before had they been seen as those who would renew ordination.[6]

The first part of the letter reads:

> First, we plead with you on behalf of the entire congregation of Israel, whose dignity has been trampled upon, and his holy name which has become desecrated, as we are asked "where is your God?" Our energy are depleted and our minds clouded and have not the strength to pray effectively before our creator as the scripture says . . . and now, in the later generations, as the tribulations are more frequent and sustenance is hard to come across . . . we thereby beseech our master, help us! Oh help us! You are our brothers, we are the sons of one man, aid us, aid us in prayer!

On October 18, 1830, Rabbi Israel signed his name to this extraordinary epistle. "The letter was given to Barukh ben Samuel of Pinsk, who was being dispatched to locate the Ten Tribes."[7]

These faithful Jewish leaders, who longed for the priesthood (of ordination) and for the ordained leaders among the ten tribes to come and lead them to the Messiah, believed their mission had failed when after four years of visiting every people he thought might have the keys he sought, Rabbi Barukh's mission ended with his murder in 1834.

But God had heard the cry of His people. He was performing His work, His great work, which would be the salvation of His people. Rabbi Israel and his fellows recognized that they needed help from someone among the lost ten tribes and that they specifically needed "ordination" in order to move forward in the gathering of all Israel together again as one in preparation to meet the Messiah.

In May 1829, a few months before Rabbi Barukh began his journey with the letter to the ten tribes, the ancient Apostles, Peter,

---

6. Arie Morgenstern, *Hastening Redemption: Messianism and the Resettlement of the Land of Israel*, 102.
7. Ibid.; see also Eli Birnbaum, *Beyond Time, Beyond Place*, jewishhistory.org.il.

James, and John, appeared to the prophet Joseph Smith near the Susquehanna River in New York State. They placed their hands upon the head of Joseph and his companion, Oliver Cowdery, and ordained them to the Melchizedek Priesthood, authorizing them to administer therein. Shortly afterward, in April 1830, The Church of Jesus Christ of Latter-day Saints was organized, beginning a new dawn for the family of covenant Israel.

CHAPTER 22

Joseph, Son of Joseph: The Lineage of Joseph Smith and the Mission of the Tribe of Joseph

Is it a coincidence that the Jerusalem rabbis were looking for a group of men who properly held the priesthood at the very time the Melchizedek Priesthood was restored to Joseph Smith, the prophet? Joseph never knew of the letter from Rabbi Israel, but God was orchestrating His work and the restoration of His people. The Lord had promised, "Behold, I, even I, will both search my sheep, and seek them out,"[1] and so, surely the eye of the Good Shepherd was upon Rabbi Israel and Rabbi Barukh and was reaching out to Joseph Smith, an Ephraimite,[2] even at the same time He was instilling the desire within the Jewish rabbis to find their lost brethren and the restoration of all the covenant blessings.

Joseph of Egypt Prophesies of Joseph Smith, His Descendant

Before his death, Joseph of Egypt prophesied concerning two great leaders that would be called by the Lord to aid the children of

1. Ezekiel 34:11.
2. *Journal of Discourses,* 2:268.

Israel. The first was the prophet Moses, whom we revere for his courage and faith. Moses is *the* great prophet who led Israel out of Egypt and bondage into the wilderness of Sinai to meet God, covenant with Him, and eventually reach the border of the promised land. Moses gathered Israel and unified them as one under covenant to God.

The second prophet that Joseph of Egypt foresaw was one that would be called in the latter days after the scattering of Israel. That prophet would be named Joseph, and his father would also be called Joseph. This latter-day prophet would do a great work in uniting the tribes of Israel, specifically by bringing them to a knowledge of the covenants made with the fathers and preparing them to meet the Messiah. This is the same work Moses did when he brought the children of Israel to Mount Sinai. There they learned about the covenant made with Adam and Eve and Abraham and Sarah, and there they were invited to enter that same covenant in an intimate encounter with Jehovah.

The latter-day Joseph was to bring his people to a knowledge of the covenants made to the fathers by bringing forth the Lord's word. In fact, the word he would bring forth would be a second witness to that word which had already gone forth through the tribe of Judah, or the Bible. That latter-day prophet was Joseph Smith, and the word he was to bring forth was the Book of Mormon, a record of a branch of Israel who had been broken off and taken to the New World. They were also a covenant people unto God.

According to Joseph of Egypt's prophecy, the goal of bringing forth the latter word, or the Book of Mormon, to accompany the Bible was to confound false doctrine, end contention, and establish peace while bringing people to a knowledge of their forefathers and the Lord's covenants.[3]

Joseph of Egypt's prophecy in its entirety follows. The first part of his prophecy concerns Moses:

> Thus saith the Lord God of my fathers unto me, A choice seer will I raise up out of the fruit of thy loins, and he shall be esteemed highly

3. See Genesis 50:30, Joseph Smith Translation.

> among the fruit of thy loins; and unto him will I give commandment that he shall do a work for the fruit of thy loins, his brethren.
>
> And he shall bring them to the knowledge of the covenants which I have made with thy fathers; and he shall do whatsoever work I shall command him.
>
> And I will make him great in mine eyes, for he shall do my work; and he shall be great like unto him whom I have said I would raise up unto you, to deliver my people, O house of Israel, out of the land of Egypt; for a seer will I raise up to deliver my people out of the land of Egypt; and he shall be called Moses. And by this name he shall know that he is of thy house; for he shall be nursed by the kings' daughter, and shall be called her son.

The next part of Joseph of Egypt's prophecy concerns a latter-day Joseph:

> And again, a seer will I raise up out of the fruit of thy loins, and unto him will I give power to bring forth my word unto the seed of my loins; and not the bringing forth of my word only, saith the Lord, but to the convincing them of my word, which shall have already gone forth among them in the last days;
>
> Wherefore the fruit of thy loins shall write, and the fruit of the loins of Judah shall write; and that which shall be written by the fruit of thy loins, and also that which shall be written by the fruit of the loins of Judah, shall grow together unto the confounding of false doctrines, and laying down contentions, and establishing peace among the fruit of thy loins, and bringing them to a knowledge of their fathers in the latter days; and also to the knowledge of my covenants, saith the Lord.
>
> And out of weakness shall he be made strong, in that day when my work shall go forth among all my people, which shall restore them, who are of the house of Israel, in the last days.
>
> And that seer will I bless, and they that seek to destroy him shall be confounded; for this promise I give unto you; for I will remember

> you from generation to generation; and his name shall be called Joseph, and it shall be after the name of his father; and he shall be like unto you; for the thing which the Lord shall bring forth by his hand shall bring my people unto salvation.[4]

Notice that one of the purposes of the latter-day Joseph's mission was to "restore the house of Israel in the last days."[5] The bringing forth of the Lord's word through the Book of Mormon would, like Moses, help gather Israel and unite the tribes as a covenant people.

Father Lehi, a Descendant of Joseph, Prophesies of Joseph Smith

Referring to Joseph of Egypt's prophecy, and following his example, Father Lehi, prior to his death in the New World, shared his final words and prophecies with his children as recorded in the Book of Mormon. To his son, Joseph, he said:

> For behold, thou art the fruit of my loins; and I am a descendant of Joseph who was carried captive into Egypt. And great were the covenants of the Lord which he made unto Joseph.
>
> Wherefore, Joseph truly saw our day. And he obtained a promise of the Lord that out of the fruit of his loins the Lord would raise up a righteous branch unto the house of Israel; not the Messiah, but a branch which was to be broken off, nevertheless, to be remembered in the covenants of the Lord that the Messiah should be made manifest unto them in the latter days, in the spirit of power, unto the bringing of them out of darkness unto light—yea, out of hidden darkness and out of captivity unto freedom.
>
> For Joseph truly testified, saying: A seer shall the Lord my God raise up, who shall be a choice seer unto the fruit of my loins.
>
> Yea, Joseph truly said: Thus saith the Lord unto me: A choice seer will I raise up out of the fruit of thy loins; and he shall be esteemed

---

4. Genesis 50:27–33, Joseph Smith Translation.
5. Genesis 50:32, Joseph Smith Translation.

highly among the fruit of thy loins. And unto him will I give commandment that he shall do a work for the fruit of thy loins, his brethren, which shall be of great worth unto them, even to the bringing of them to the knowledge of the covenants which I have made with thy fathers.

And I will give unto him a commandment that he shall do none other work, save the work which I shall command him. And I will make him great in mine eyes; for he shall do my work.

And he shall be great like unto Moses, whom I have said I would raise up unto you, to deliver my people, O house of Israel.

And Moses will I raise up, to deliver thy people out of the land of Egypt.

But a seer will I raise up out of the fruit of thy loins; and unto him will I give power to bring forth my word unto the seed of thy loins—and not to the bringing forth my word only, saith the Lord, but to the convincing them of my word, which shall have already gone forth among them.

Wherefore, the fruit of thy loins shall write; and the fruit of the loins of Judah shall write; and that which shall be written by the fruit of thy loins, and also that which shall be written by the fruit of the loins of Judah, shall grow together, unto the confounding of false doctrines and laying down of contentions, and establishing peace among the fruit of thy loins, and bringing them to the knowledge of their fathers in the latter days, and also to the knowledge of my covenants, saith the Lord.

And out of weakness he shall be made strong, in that day when my work shall commence among all my people, unto the restoring thee, O house of Israel, saith the Lord.

And thus prophesied Joseph, saying: Behold, that seer will the Lord bless; and they that seek to destroy him shall be confounded; for this promise, which I have obtained of the Lord, of the fruit of my loins, shall be fulfilled. Behold, I am sure of the fulfilling of this promise;

And his name shall be called after me; and it shall be after the name of his father. And he shall be like unto me; for the thing, which the Lord shall bring forth by his hand, by the power of the Lord shall bring my people unto salvation.

Yea, thus prophesied Joseph: I am sure of this thing, even as I am sure of the promise of Moses; for the Lord hath said unto me, I will preserve thy seed forever.

. . . And the Lord said unto me also: I will raise up unto the fruit of thy loins; and I will make for him a spokesman. And I, behold, I will give unto him that he shall write the writing of the fruit of thy loins, unto the fruit of thy loins; and the spokesman of thy loins shall declare it.

And the words which he shall write shall be the words which are expedient in my wisdom should go forth unto the fruit of thy loins. And it shall be as if the fruit of thy loins had cried unto them from the dust; for I know their faith.

And they shall cry from the dust; yea, even repentance unto their brethren, even after many generations have gone by them. And it shall come to pass that their cry shall go, even according to the simpleness of their words.

Because of their faith their words shall proceed forth out of my mouth unto their brethren who are the fruit of thy loins; and the weakness of their words will I make strong in their faith, unto the remembering of my covenant which I made unto thy fathers.

. . . And there shall rise up one mighty among them, who shall do much good, both in word and in deed, being an instrument in the hands of God, with exceeding faith, to work mighty wonders, and do that thing which is great in the sight of God, unto the bringing to pass much restoration unto the house of Israel, and unto the seed of thy brethren.[6]

6. 2 Nephi 3:4–24.

Joseph Smith Was Both Gentile and Israelite (Tribe of Joseph)

Brigham Young declared that Joseph Smith was a "pure Ephraimite."[7]

The information as to what tribe an individual is from is typically revealed through a patriarchal blessing where the patriarch's main focus is in declaring the lineage of the person receiving the blessing.

Daniel Ludlow sheds light on the subject of Brigham's declaration regarding Joseph Smith's lineage. He noted that

> So far as the Prophet's family or blood lines were concerned, Brigham Young and others have recognized that 1) Joseph Smith was from a Gentile nation, and 2) some of Joseph Smith's progenitors may have come from bloodlines other than that of Ephraim.[8]

While we recognize that the ten tribes were dispersed throughout the ancient world, including Europe, we note that for the most part, they lost remembrance of their identity as the House of Israel. They mingled with other nations, resulting in mixed bloodlines. It's important to recognize that this is part of God's plan and not an accident where He somehow lost track of His people.

Joseph Fielding Smith explained that

> The Lord said he would scatter Israel among the Gentile nations, and by doing so he would bless the Gentile nations with the blood of Abraham. Today we are preaching the gospel in the world and we are gathering out, according to the revelations given to Isaiah, Jeremiah, and other prophets, the scattered sheep of the House of Israel. These scattered sheep are coming forth mixed with Gentile blood from their Gentile forefathers. Under all the circumstances it is very possible that the majority, almost without exception, of those who come into the Church in this dispensation have the blood of two or more of the tribes of Israel as well as the blood of the Gentiles.[9]

---

7. *Journal of Discourses*, 2:268–69.
8. Daniel H. Ludlow, "Of the House of Israel," *Ensign*, January 1991.
9. Joseph Fielding Smith, *Answers to Gospel Questions*, 3:63.

Whether a person has one or more of the tribes of Israel as part of their heritage, or if they have all Gentile forebears, "all are alike unto God,"[10] and all are invited to enter the covenant of Israel and receive of those sacred blessings.

The patriarchal blessing that assigns each individual to a tribe of Israel is designating the role of the singular tribe to which that person is assigned, even if they have the DNA of several tribes. Thus, Joseph Smith, though both Gentile and Israelite, was assigned to the tribe of Ephraim (and called a pure Ephraimite) simply due to the specific role that the tribe of Ephraim is to play in the last days.

Joseph Fielding Smith explained that

> Every person who embraces the gospel becomes of the house of Israel. In other words, they become members of the chosen lineage, or Abraham's children through Isaac and Jacob unto whom the promises were made. The great majority of those who become members of the Church are literal descendants of Abraham through Ephraim, son of Joseph. Those who are not literal descendants of Abraham and Israel must become such, and when they are baptized and confirmed they are grafted into the tree and are entitled to all the rights and privileges as heirs.[11]

Joseph Smith (and many of us) play a dual role as both Gentile and House of Israel. Joseph Fielding Smith taught that

> In this Dispensation of the Fulness of Times, the gospel came first to the Gentiles and then is to go to the Jews. However, the Gentiles who receive the gospel are, in the greater part, Gentiles who have the blood of Israel in their veins. There is a very significant statement in the words of Moroni as recorded on the title page of the Book of Mormon that it was "To come forth . . . by way of the Gentile."
>
> How did the Book of Mormon come forth? By the hand of Joseph Smith. Yet we read in the Book of Mormon (see 2 Ne. 3:7–15)

10. 2 Nephi 26:33.
11. Joseph Fielding Smith, *Doctrines of Salvation*, 3:246.

> that Joseph Smith is the descendant of Joseph of who was sold into Egypt by his brethren, nevertheless he came by "way of the Gentile," according to Moroni's prediction.[12]

This "mixing" of Gentile and Israelite blood is important in illustrating how important it is for us to tear down the artificial walls that separate us from recognizing our brotherhood and sisterhood as children of God. Even as Peter had to put aside his belief that the covenant was meant only for the Jews when God prepared him to meet and baptize the Roman Cornelius,[13] so the Gentiles must put aside their animosity toward those of Israel, primarily seen today as the Jews (or any other race).

Ephraim (and Manasseh) to Gather Israel and Restore the Covenant

As illustrated by Joseph Smith—whom Joseph Fielding Smith referred to as both Gentile and Ephraimite—the tribe of Joseph, through Ephraim, is now stepping forward into the long-prophesied role as one who saves and gathers Israel by bringing them back to the covenant.

Moses had prophesied:

> Let the blessing come upon the head of Joseph, and upon the top of the head of him that was separated from his brethren. His glory is like the firstling of his bullock, and his horns are like the horns of unicorns [Hebrew: the wild ox]: with them he shall push the people together to the ends of the earth: and they are the ten thousands of Ephraim, and they are the thousands of Manasseh.[14]

Anciently, Joseph was marked as the birthright son, who with the responsibility of the priesthood had the responsibility to care for his family and provide for their needs. Even though his brothers thought

12. Joseph Fielding Smith, *Answers to Gospel Questions*, 4:39.
13. See Acts 10.
14. Deuteronomy 33:16–17.

of that assignment purely in worldly terms and destroyed the coat and sold Joseph into Egypt, God affirmed Joseph's priesthood assignment and sent him ahead to care and provide for his family. This Joseph did without any sign of rancor or resentment. Those who are of the tribe of Joseph today are set apart to fulfill the same role: to be the caretakers who provide the sustenance of covenant power, priesthood, and ordinances to the entire house of Israel.

Rabbi Israel and his fellows recognized the important role of someone from the tribe of Joseph or Ephraim who would have the "ordination" necessary to unite with his Jewish brothers and help gather and prepare Israel for the coming Messiah. Rabbi Israel was right, although he did not know of Joseph Smith.

Moses foresaw that Ephraim and Manasseh (counted as one tribe with their father Joseph) would have the responsibility of gathering Israel again. The symbol for both Ephraim and Manasseh is the wild ox, the same as the symbol of the twelve oxen supporting a sea of water in both the ancient and modern temple. In the modern temple, we interpret that sea as the waters of baptism through which one enters into covenant with the Lord, takes upon themselves the name of Jesus Christ, and becomes a member of the House of Israel.

Jeffrey Bradshaw encourages:

> Just as the blessing of Judah will have its ultimate fulfillment in the second coming of the Messiah in His glory, so the greatest prophecies of the blessing of Joseph will come to pass through the gathering of Israel in the last days. This means that the primary significance of the declaration of lineage in one's patriarchal blessing is not in its assertion of eventual, conditional blessings, but rather in its reminder of our immediate responsibilities to assist with that gathering—on behalf of both the living and those who have passed on.[15]

As foreshadowed by his ancestor Joseph of Egypt, Joseph Smith was the restorer from Ephraim meant to unify the tribes of Israel. One of the main tools of that restoration and unification is the Book of

---

15. Jeffrey Bradshaw, "How Should We Understand the Rich Symbolism in Jacob's Blessings of Judah and Joseph?," *Meridian Magazine*, 2018.

Mormon, a second witness to the Bible, the book of the Jews, preserved and cherished despite the sufferings and hardships they have endured. Together the two books bear witness of the love of God and the Plan of Salvation.

CHAPTER 23

The Stick of Judah and the Stick of Joseph

Ezekiel's Vision of Dry Bones

In the midst of his revelation of dry, dead bones being brought back to life, the ancient prophet Ezekiel included the following:

> Moreover thou son of man, take thee one stick, and write upon it, For Judah, and for the children of Israel his companions: then take another stick, and write upon it, For Joseph, the stick of Ephraim, and for all the house of Israel his companions: And join them one to another into one stick; and they shall become one in thine hand.
>
> And when the children of thy people shall speak unto thee, saying, Wilt thou not shew us what thou meanest by these? Say unto them, Thus saith the Lord God; Behold, I will take the stick of Joseph, which is in the hand of Ephraim, and the tribes of Israel his fellows, and I will put them with him, even with the stick of Judah, and make them one stick, and they shall be one in mine hand. And the sticks whereon thou writest shall be in thine hand before their eyes.[1]

1. Ezekiel 37:16–20.

Ezekiel had been taken captive by the Babylonians during their second attack against Jerusalem. He taught and prophesied among the captives near the river Chebar.

The context of the revelation regarding the two sticks—one for Judah and one for Joseph—was in the midst of a vision wherein Ezekiel saw a valley of dry bones that symbolized the death of Israel. In the vision, God asked Ezekiel if he believed that the bones could live again. The Lord then clarified, "Son of man, these bones are the whole house of Israel: behold, they say, Our bones are dried, and our hope is lost: we are cut off for our parts."[2]

According to the vision, Israel felt that all hope was lost, yet the Lord breathed life upon them and the bones took on skin, sinew, and life. The Lord then promised:

> Behold, O my people, I will open your graves, and cause you to come up out of your graves, and bring you into the land of Israel. And ye shall know that I am the Lord, when I have opened your graves, O my people, and brought you up out of your graves. And shall put my spirit in you, and ye shall live, and I shall place you in your own land: then shall ye know that I the Lord have spoken it, and performed *it*, saith the Lord.[3]

Then, at that moment in the vision, when you can almost hear the question "*How? How can this be accomplished when all is lost and Israel is banished?*," the Lord speaks about the two sticks, one for Judah and one for Joseph, that shall be joined as one. The Lord anticipates the question about what the two sticks might have to do with the promise of Israel's restoration, and He answers:

> And say unto them, Thus saith the Lord God; Behold, I will take the children of Israel from among the heathen, wither they be gone, and will gather them on every side, and bring them into their own land: And I will make them one nation in the land upon the mountains of Israel; and one king shall be king to them all: and they

2. Ezekiel 37:11.
3. Ezekiel 37:12–14.

> shall be no more two nations, neither shall they be divided into two kingdoms any more at all.[4]

Sticks, Books, and Wood Tablets

Critics of the interpretation that the two sticks represent two books—the Bible and the Book of Mormon—are quick to point out that the Hebrew root of the word "stick" or *'aytz* is clearly *wood.* They insist that Ezekiel's meaning was that he was to take a plank of wood representing the northern tribes under Ephraim (or Joseph) and write that name upon it. He was to do likewise for Judah, and then holding the two planks with his hand joining them in the center, one above, and one below, represent the return of Israel to her northern and southern lands.[5]

Latter-day Saint scholars have long acknowledged that *'aytz* indeed does means *wood.* In a 1987 article in the *Ensign*, Keith Meservy wrote:

> We must look at Ezekiel's use of his wood (*'ets)* [or *'aytz*] in chapter 37 to determine its meaning. Ezekiel *wrote* on his wood . . . Since archaeologists know now that ancient Babylonians wrote on wood, this knowledge provides a valuable context within which to interpret the meaning of Ezekiel's action.[6]

Meservy goes on to explain that Babylonian scribes wrote on wooden tablets that were often joined by hinges. The scribes wrote directly upon the wood in cuneiform, or on wax that had been poured over the planks.[7]

Meservy quotes the New English Bible translation of the same verses as saying:

> These were the words of the Lord to me: Man, *take one leaf of a wooden tablet* and write on it, "Judah and his associates of Israel." Then take another leaf and write on it, "Joseph, the leaf of Ephraim

---

4. Ezekiel 37: 21–22.
5. Jews for Judaism, "The Stick of Judah and the Stick of Joseph."
6. Keith Meservy, "Ezekiel's Sticks and the Gathering of Israel," *Ensign,* February 1987.
7. Ibid.

> and all of his associates of Israel." Now bring the two together to form one tablet; then they will be a folding tablet in your hand. These are the words of the Lord God: I am taking the leaf of Joseph, *which belongs to* Ephraim and his associate tribes of Israel, and joining it to the leaf of Judah. Thus I shall make them one tablet.[8]

The authors at Faithful Answers, Informed Responses (FAIR) add, "The sticks, of course, are records or books. In ancient Israel records were written upon tablets of wood or scrolls rolled upon sticks."[9]

Healing and Unity

Note that the vision of the two books is associated with the vision of returning life to Israel, Israel's gathering, and the promise that the joining together of the two books will bring unity to the two kingdoms or tribes of Judah and Joseph. This is a powerful promise and reason to be keenly interested in finding and embracing the stick of Joseph (because the stick of Judah has already been identified as the Bible).

Please also note that the Ezekiel prophecy refers also to the other tribes of Israel and not just to Judah and Joseph. To Judah, Ezekiel is to add "the children of Israel his companions"[10] and to Joseph, he is to add "the tribes of Israel his fellows."[11] As has been previously stated here, the tribes of Judah and Joseph represented the two leading tribes of Israel. Judah also incorporated Benjamin and any other individuals and families who wanted to maintain the purity of temple worship in Jerusalem after Jeroboam divided the kingdom. Joseph, through Ephraim, represented the ten tribes to the north in what was called the Northern Kingdom. All tribes are represented in the promise of the unifying and restoration that will result as the two books are joined as one in the hand of the Lord.

---

8. Keith Meservy, "Ezekiel's Sticks and the Gathering of Israel," *Ensign,* February 1987.
9. "The Book of Mormon and the Stick of Ephraim," Faithful Answers, Informed Responses, fairlatterdaysaints.org.
10. Ezekiel 37:16.
11. Ezekiel 37:19.

Appreciating Both Books— The Bible and the Book of Mormon

Sadly, the writer of an essay on Jews for Judaism accuses the Latter-day Saints of not demonstrating much esteem for the Bible. The writer questions why the Latter-day Saints place so much emphasis on the Ezekiel prophecy of the two sticks when they don't pay much attention to the Bible.[12] Frankly, comments made during a typical Old Testament year of study in the rotating curriculum in Gospel Doctrine could add credibility to that statement.

In a talk called "The Miracle of the Holy Bible," M. Russell Ballard urged:

> Honest, diligent study of the Bible does make us better and better, and we must ever remember the countless martyrs who knew of its power and who gave their lives that we may be able to find within its words the path to the eternal happiness and the peace of our Heavenly Father's kingdom.[13]

Elder Ballard goes on to say:

> Those who join this Church do not give up their faith in the Bible—they strengthen it. The Book of Mormon does not dilute nor diminish nor de-emphasize the Bible. On the contrary, it expands, extends, and exalts it. The Book of Mormon testifies of the Bible, and both testify of Christ.
>
> The first testament of Christ is the Bible's Old Testament, which predicted and prophesied of the coming of the Savior, His transcendent life, and His liberating Atonement. The second Bible testament of Christ is the New Testament, which records His birth, His life, His ministry, His gospel, His Church, His Atonement, and His Resurrection, as well as the testimonies of His Apostles. The third testament of Christ is the Book of Mormon, which also foretells Christ's coming, confirms the Bible's account of His saving Atonement, and then reveals the resurrected Lord's visit to the earth's other hemisphere. The subtitle of the Book of Mormon, the clarifying purpose statement printed on the cover of

---

12. Jews for Judaism, "The Stick of Judah and the Stick of Joseph."
13. M. Russell Ballard, "The Miracle of the Bible," *Ensign*, May 2007.

every copy, is "Another Testament of Jesus Christ." Each of these three testaments is a part of the great, indivisible whole of the Lord's revealed word to His children. They contain the words of Christ, which we have been admonished to feast upon as a means of qualifying for eternal life (see 2 Nephi 31:20). *Those who think that one part is more important or more true than the other parts are missing some of the beauty and completeness of the canon of ancient scripture.*[14]

The ancient prophet Nephi warned that prejudice might go in the other direction as well. Those who loved the Bible might reject the Book of Mormon. Through Nephi, the Lord asked:

> Wherefore murmur ye, because that ye shall receive more of my word? Know ye not that the testimony of two nations is a witness unto you that I am God, that I remember one nation like unto another? Wherefore, I speak the same words unto one nation like unto another. And when the two nations shall run together the testimony of the two nations shall run together also.[15]

Isn't it reassuring to know that God is working with and communicating with His children wherever they may be throughout the world? In the same instruction to Nephi, the Lord said that He is having additional nations write their records as well. We can look forward to seeing the records of the other various tribes of Israel who have been lost or scattered and rejoice in knowing that all have the same word from God and a reminder of His loving covenant promises.

> For behold, I shall speak unto the Jews and they shall write it; and I shall also speak unto the Nephites and they shall write it [the Book of Mormon]; and I shall also speak unto the other tribes of the house of Israel, which I have led away, and they shall write it; and I shall also speak unto all nations of the earth and they shall write it. And it shall come to pass that the Jews shall have the words of the Nephites, and the Nephites shall have the words of the Jews; and the Nephites and the Jews shall have the words of the lost tribes of Israel; and the lost tribes of Israel shall have the words of the Nephites and the Jews. And

---

14. M. Russell Ballard, "The Miracle of the Bible," *Ensign*, May 2007; emphasis added.
15. 2 Nephi 29:8.

> it shall come to pass that my people, which are of the house of Israel, shall be gathered home unto the lands of their possessions; and my word also shall be gathered in one.[16]

The Book of Mormon a Sign of the Gathering of Israel

The plates that contained what we call the Book of Mormon were removed from the Hill Cumorah by Joseph Smith on September 22, 1823. It was the ancient Israelite feast day of Rosh Hashanah, the Feast of Trumpets.

Rosh Hashanah marks a new year on the Israelite calendar. (There are two new years, the other is Pesach, or Passover.) The blowing of the trumpets associated with the feast signals to Israel to "Awake!" and prepare for the Day of Atonement (Yom Kippur) ten days later by participating in a time of reflection and repentance. The Day of Atonement is the holiest day of the year when it is believed that one's name is written in the Book of Life or Death. This ten-day period between Trumpets and the Day of Atonement is referred to as "the Days of Awe," when one turns one's heart to God and seeks to restore that relationship to honest wholeness. The sacrifice of the scapegoat on the Day of Atonement underscores the importance of confessing one's sins and receiving an atonement for them.

The Feast of Trumpets is also the beginning of the fall feasts, signaling a time to gather in not only the crops of the field, but also all of Israel preparatory to the final fall feast, Sukkot, or The Feast of Tabernacles. These three fall feasts—Rosh Hashanah (Trumpets), Yom Kippur (Day of Atonement), and Sukkot (Tabernacles) are considered the most joyous of all of the feasts because they anticipate the gathering of Israel in preparation to meet her Messiah.[17]

Because the Lord chose to bring the Book of Mormon forth on the Feast of Trumpets, it is important to consider how it meets or fulfills the principles of the fall feasts. Moroni, who led Joseph Smith to the plates at Cumorah, is today represented as having a trumpet in his mouth, even in the act of blowing the trumpet. Could the Book of Mormon be issuing the same call to "Awake!," consider our standing

---

16. 2 Nephi 29:12–14.
17. See Lynda Cherry's *The Feasts and Festivals of the Messiah.*

before God, confess and repent of our sins, and prepare ourselves for the day we will meet with the Messiah again? Surely, it does fulfill all of these criteria.

In addition, the fall feasts were considered the time of the ingathering of Israel. Does the Book of Mormon speak to that?

Russell M. Nelson taught:

> This doctrine of the gathering is one of the important teachings of The Church of Jesus Christ of Latter-day Saints. The Lord has declared: "I give unto you a sign . . . that I shall gather in, from their long dispersion, my people, O house of Israel, and shall establish again among them my Zion" (3 Nephi 21:1). The coming forth of the Book of Mormon is a sign to the entire world that the Lord has commenced to gather Israel and fulfill covenants He made to Abraham, Isaac, and Jacob.[18]

Anciently, Moses was sent by the Lord to gather His people Israel and take them to the land promised to Abraham and Sarah, Isaac and Rebekah, Jacob and Rachel, and Leah. Today, the Book of Mormon also plays the role of a gatherer, or at least, a gathering tool. The Lord told Nephi:

> And it shall come to pass that my people, which are of the house of Israel, shall be gathered home unto the lands of their possessions; and my word also shall be gathered in one. And I will show unto them that fight against my word and against my people, who are of the house of Israel, that I am God, and that I covenanted with Abraham that I would remember his seed forever.[19]

---

18. Russell M. Nelson, "The Gathering of Scattered Israel," *Ensign*, November 2006.
19. 2 Nephi 29:14.

CHAPTER 24

To Judah from Joseph: The Kirtland Temple Prayer and the Dedication of the Holy Land

How beautiful upon the mountains
are the feet of him that bringeth good tidings,
that publisheth peace;
that bringeth good tidings of good,
that publisheth salvation;
that saith unto Zion, Thy God reigneth![1]

ISAIAH PROPHESIED OF A FUTURE DAY WHEN JERUSALEM AND HER people would "awake . . . put on her beautiful garments . . . arise and sit down . . . and loose herself from the bands" of captivity.[2] Jehovah would send messengers beforehand, bringing the "good tidings of good," the assurance that salvation was near and that Israel's God was still present, watching and reigning over His people. Isaiah described the resultant songs of joy that would burst forth voluntarily when Israel realizes this great truth: that the covenant still stands, that God remembers, and that He is bringing salvation.

1. Isaiah 52:7.
2. Isaiah 52:1–2.

Joseph Smith Recognizes the Jews as a Covenant People

Joseph Smith was raised at a time of a great Christian religious revival known as the Second Great Awakening. The spirit of evangelism ruled the day, with each church seeking for its own converts and claiming superiority over the others. Joseph Smith wrote that these efforts "created no small stir and division among the people, some crying, 'Lo, here!' And others, 'Lo, there!' "[3] This confusion and contention affected Joseph's own family and led to his determination to pray and ask God which of all the churches he should join.[4]

It's interesting to note that despite having been raised in this religious environment of proselytizing and contention between the sects, Joseph Smith is noted for his respect and regard for the Jews and did not seek to convert them after the formation of The Church of Jesus Christ of Latter-day Saints.

Joseph's regard for the Jews is notable in the changes that took place in the newspaper *Times and Seasons* once he became its editor. With the very first issue under his purview, Joseph published an article written by a Jew on the subject of what it felt like to be a Jew living among American Christians. Joseph titled the anonymous article, "A word in season from an Israelite, to his brethren" and added no commentary or editorial notes to it, allowing the sentiments and beliefs of the author to speak entirely for himself.[5]

Steven Epperson notes that

> Throughout his career [Joseph Smith] turned to Israel's institutions, categories, and practices to distinguish the Latter-day Saints from Christendom and to underline Mormon continuity with covenant Israel. Having "translated" the Book of Mormon, and being cognizant of that text's belief that law and doctrine had proceeded forth "in purity" from "the Jews" before Christian designs had distorted the scriptural canon, perhaps Joseph was now providing a limited forum for Israel's voice to again edify the Saints.[6]

---

3. Joseph Smith—History 1:5.
4. Joseph Smith—History 1:7–12.
5. Steven Epperson, "Jews in the Columns of Joseph's *Times and Seasons*," dialoguejournal.com.
6. Ibid.

Joseph Smith published numerous articles written by Jewish sources, often without any editorial comments. Once, Joseph published an extract from an essay by Rabbi Sampson Raphael Hirsch, the founder of contemporary Orthodox Judaism, titled "Horeb: Essays on Israel's Duties in the Dispersion." Joseph added the following comment: "Jews . . . maintain principles of benevolence and charity which many of our professed enlightened Christians would do well to imitate."[7]

As the founder of The Church of Jesus Christ of Latter-day Saints, Joseph Smith stands out from his contemporaries in his teachings and attitude toward the Jewish people.

> In sum, he denounced Christian anti-Jewish bias, repudiated programmatic evangelization of the Jewish people, and denied the corporate guilt and punishment traditionally assigned the Jews for the death of Jesus of Nazareth. In sermons, scriptures, periodicals, and encounters with Jewish contemporaries, Joseph sought to rehabilitate Christian theological and historical judgments of Jewry, Judaism, and Jewish institutions of both the past and the present.[8]

Prayer for the Jews at the Kirtland Temple Dedication

The fact that Joseph Smith felt a kinship with the Jewish people is evidenced not only in the articles published in *The Times and Seasons*, but also in his discourses, his determination to learn Hebrew, and particularly, in his prayer for the Jews at the dedication of the Kirtland Temple.

It may be that Joseph's love for the ancient covenant family came from those days in his youth, when surrounded by his parents and siblings, they conversed about what they were reading in the Bible. It may be that the love for Israel was transferred directly through the Spirit and Joseph's encounter with deity. Or, it may be that Moroni's initial scripture-quoting impacted Joseph as he reviewed those same Old Testament prophecies concerning the ancient covenant people.

---

7. *Times and Seasons*, March 15, 1842 edition, as quoted by Steven Epperson, "Jews in the Columns of Joseph's *Times and Seasons*," dialoguejournal.com.
8. Steven Epperson, "Jews in the Columns of Joseph's *Times and Seasons*," dialoguejournal.com.

Imagine Joseph as a young teen, overwhelmed by the appearance of an angel in the middle of the night, telling him that he had a work to do![9] Wouldn't that work be stamped into the very fibers of his being? If the scriptures Moroni had quoted would help Joseph understand and prepare himself for that work, surely he would have reviewed them frequently.

The first scripture that Joseph recorded as having received from Moroni was from the third chapter of Malachi, which Joseph noted that Moroni quoted differently than as recorded in the current Old Testament. How important that "difference" is in content!

> Behold, I will reveal unto you the Priesthood, by the hand of Elijah the prophet, before the coming of the great and dreadful day of the Lord. . . . And he shall plant in the hearts of the children the promises made to the fathers, and the hearts of the children shall turn to their fathers. If it were not so, the whole earth would be utterly wasted at his coming.[10]

Who were the fathers if not the ancient covenant people or the family of Israel, and what were the promises made to them if not the promises of scattering, gathering, and redemption? No wonder Joseph's heart turned to the Jews with such compassion and desire.

After quoting several Old Testament passages to lay his foundation, Joseph Smith stated the following in a letter to an editor in January, 1833:

> Judah shall obtain deliverance at Jerusalem. These are testimonies that the Good Shepherd will put forth His own sheep, and lead them out from all nations where they have been scattered in a cloudy and dark day, to Zion, and to Jerusalem.[11]

Joseph Smith was eager for the prophecies to be fulfilled, and he offered himself to God as an instrument in that work.

Great sacrifice, consecration, and joy went into the construction of the first temple of this dispensation, the Kirtland Temple in Kirtland, Ohio. The temple itself was a visible and concrete link between the old

9. Joseph Smith—History 1:33.
10. Joseph Smith—History 1:36–39.
11. Joseph Smith, *History of the Church*, 1:315.

and the new, the ancient covenant people, and the newly discovered remnant as well as the newly adopted family of Israel. The ensign was being raised, and Israel was rising with it.

Isaiah had prophesied:

> And in that day there shall be a root of Jesse, which shall stand for an ensign of the people; to it shall the Gentiles seek: and his rest shall be glorious . . . And he shall set up an ensign for the nations, and shall assemble the outcasts of Israel, and gather together the dispersed of Judah from the four corners of the earth.[12]

These prophecies had undoubtedly pressed upon Joseph Smith's mind as he sought to know the work the Lord would have him do. It's not surprising then that Joseph, in his first words of the temple's dedicatory prayer in March 1836, clearly linked the temple with its purpose of uniting and saving all of Israel: "Thanks be to thy name, O Lord God of Israel, who keepest covenant and showest mercy unto thy servants who walk uprightly before thee, with all their hearts."[13] Joseph knew that the God of Israel would keep His covenants with His people.

The hoped-for salvation of Israel was clearly stated in the midst of the dedicatory prayer as Joseph pled:

> Now these words, O Lord, we have spoken before thee, concerning the revelations and commandments which thou hast given unto us, who are identified with the Gentiles. But thou knowest that thou hast a great love for the children of Jacob, who have been scattered upon the mountains for a long time, in a cloudy and dark day. We therefore ask thee to have mercy upon the children of Jacob, that Jerusalem, from this hour, may begin to be redeemed; and the yoke of bondage may be broken off from the house of David; and the children of Judah may begin to return to the lands which thou didst give to Abraham, their father.[14]

In answer to the prophetic plea, both Elijah and Moses appeared with keys of restoration at the Kirtland Temple. As promised, Elijah's

---

12. Isaiah 11:10, 12.
13. Doctrine and Covenants 109:1.
14. Doctrine and Covenants 109:60–64.

keys were sealing keys to unite the hearts of the children to those who had gone before, embracing the New and Everlasting Covenant, and calling to remembrance those great covenantal obligations and blessings.[15] Moses committed the keys of the gathering of Israel from the four parts of the earth to Joseph Smith and The Church of Jesus Christ of Latter-day Saints.[16]

An ensign had been raised—a banner of intent—that was, at the time, little understood as the Saints struggled for subsistence against persecution not unlike that of the Jews, though admittedly on a smaller scale. Despite the constant need that each day presented, Joseph Smith and his appointed leaders did not lose sight of the promises to those who lived outside of their immediate circle, specifically those promises made to the remnants of the tribe of Judah and the restoration of Jerusalem.

Orson Hyde and the Dedication of the Holy Land

Joseph Smith, as we have discussed, was vocal in his support for the Jews and their return to Jerusalem. Church members and nonmembers alike knew his position. Joseph encouraged them to join in the important work. In early November 1831, more than four years prior to the Kirtland Temple dedication, Joseph Smith gave a revelatory blessing to new convert Orson Hyde, stating that Orson was to "proclaim the everlasting gospel, by the Spirit of the living God, from people to people, and from land to land . . . in their synagogues."[17] It was the first forewarning of what would be Orson's deep involvement in the work of gathering, specifically for the tribe of Judah.

Sometime later, yet still prior to the Kirtland Temple dedication, Joseph Smith pronounced this blessing upon Orson:

> In due time thou shalt go to Jerusalem, the land of thy fathers, and be a watchman unto the house of Israel; and by thy hands shall the

15. Doctrine and Covenants 2; 110:13–15.
16. Doctrine and Covenants 110:11.
17. Doctrine and Covenants 68:1.

> Most High do a great work, which shall prepare the way and greatly facilitate the gathering together of that people.[18]

Orson recorded that later, as he lay pondering on his bed, he had a vision wherein the Lord showed him "the cities of London, Amsterdam, Constantinople and Jerusalem" and instructed him "here are the many children of Abraham whom I will gather to the land that I gave to their fathers; and here also is the field of your labors."[19]

During the April 1840 general conference of the Church, Orson Hyde received his official call and commission to go to Palestine and dedicate the land for the return of the Jewish people.[20]

It was a dangerous and difficult journey. Orson's mission companion deserted him, he had only snails to eat for many days, and he encountered unrest and murder on the streets of Beirut. He left for the mission in the fall of 1840 and arrived in Jerusalem on October 21, 1841, one year later. With an eye single to his purpose, Orson determined that he would climb the Mount of Olives on Sunday morning, October 24, and offer the following prayer of dedication:

> Now, O Lord! Thy servant has been obedient to the heavenly vision which Thou gavest him in his native land; and under the shadow of Thine outstretched arm, he has safely arrived in this place to dedicate and consecrate this land unto Thee, for the gathering together of Judah's scattered remnants, according to the predictions of the holy Prophets—for the building up of Jerusalem again after it has been trodden down by the Gentiles so long, and for rearing a Temple in honor of Thy name . . .
>
> . . . O Thou, Who didst covenant with Abraham, Thy friend, and who didst renew that covenant with Isaac, and confirm the same with Jacob with an oath, that Thou wouldst not only give them this land for an everlasting inheritance, but that Thou wouldst also remember their seed forever. Abraham, Isaac, and Jacob have long since closed their eyes in death, and made the grave their mansion. Their children are scattered and dispersed abroad among the

18. Joseph Smith, *History of the Church,* 4:375.
19. Joseph Smith, *History of the Church,* 4:375–76.
20. David Galbraith, "Orson Hyde's 1841 Mission to the Holy Land," *Ensign,* October 1991.

nations of the Gentiles like sheep that have no shepherd, and are still looking forward for the fulfillment of those promises which Thou didst make concerning them . . .

Grant, therefore, O Lord, in the name of Thy well-beloved Son, Jesus Christ, to remove the barrenness and sterility of this land, and let springs of living water break forth to water its thirsty soil. Let the vine and olive produce in their strength, and the fig-tree bloom and flourish. Let the land become abundantly fruitful when possessed by its rightful heirs; let it again flow with plenty to feed the returning prodigals who come home with a spirit of grace and supplication; upon it let the clouds distill virtue and richness, and let the fields smile with plenty. Let the flocks and the herds greatly increase and multiply upon the mountains and the hills; and let Thy great kindness conquer and subdue the unbelief of Thy people. Do Thou take from them their stony heart, and give them a heart of flesh; and may the Sun of Thy favor dispel the cold mists of darkness which have beclouded their atmosphere. Incline them to gather in upon this land according to Thy word. Let them come like clouds and like doves to their windows. Let the large ships of the nations bring them from the distant isles; and let kings become their nursing fathers, and queens with motherly fondness wipe the tear of sorrow from their eye.

Thou, O Lord, did once move upon the heart of Cyrus to show favor unto Jerusalem and her children. Do Thou now also be pleased to inspire the hearts of kings and the powers of the earth to look with a friendly eye toward this place, and with a desire to see Thy righteous purposes executed in relation thereto. Let them know that it is Thy good pleasure to restore the kingdom unto Israel—raise up Jerusalem as its capital, and constitute her people a distinct nation and government, with David Thy servant, even a descendant from the loins of ancient David to be their king.

Let that nation or that people who shall take an active part in behalf of Abraham's children, and in the raising up of Jerusalem, find favor in Thy sight. Let not their enemies prevail against them, neither let pestilence or famine overcome them, but let the glory of Israel overshadow them, and the power of the Highest protect them; while that nation or kingdom that will not serve Thee in this glorious

> work must perish, according to Thy word—Yea, those nations shall be utterly wasted . . .
>
> . . . Do Thou arise in the majesty of Thy strength, and make bare Thine arm in behalf of Thy people. Redress their wrongs, and turn their sorrow into joy. Pour the spirit of light and knowledge, grace and wisdom, into the hearts of her Prophets, and clothe her Priests with salvation. Let light and knowledge march forth through the empire of darkness, and may the honest in heart flow to their standard, and join in the march to go forth to meet the Bridegroom.[21]

Orson recorded that he erected "a pile of stones as a witness according to ancient custom" on both the Mount of Olives and Mount Moriah "where the temple [had] stood."[22]

The Jews Make a Homeland in Jerusalem

David Galbraith wrote:

> It is no coincidence that historical annals point to the 1840s as a period of awakening among Jews dispersed throughout the world. Out of this new dawn arose men of influence like Moses Hess, Joseph Salvador, Moses Montefiore, Leo Pinsker, and Theodor Herzl. Having been touched by the spirit of gathering, they began to instill in Jews everywhere the desire to return to their ancient homeland. At first, Jews began returning by the hundreds. But eventually they were returning by thousands and then by tens and hundreds of thousands.[23]

After their long dispersion, the Jews formed the state of Israel in 1948, almost exactly one hundred years following Elder Hyde's dedication. The last time they had been an independent entity was during Isaiah's lifetime—before the Assyrian and Babylonian conquests.

---

21. Joseph Smith, *History of the Church*, 4:456–59.
22. Ibid.
23. David Galbraith, "Orson Hyde's 1841 Mission to the Holy Land," *Ensign*, October 1991.

Isaiah had prophesied "Comfort ye, comfort ye my people, saith your God. Speak ye comfortably to Jerusalem, and cry unto her, that her warfare is accomplished, that her iniquity is pardoned."[24]

There have been many others in addition to Orson Hyde who have sought to "speak comfortably" in reassurance to Jerusalem and to the Jews. Ten dedicatory prayers have been offered in addition to Hyde's that have been performed over a sixty-year period (1873–1933),[25] indicating the unique interest and concern for the tribe of Judah and its associates by the tribe of Joseph as represented by The Church of Jesus Christ of Latter-day Saints.[26]

---

24. Isaiah 40:1–2.
25. Blair G. VanDyke and LaMar C. Barrett, "In the Footsteps of Orson Hyde: Subsequent Dedications of the Holy Land."
26. David Galbraith explains, "It was perhaps inevitable that the gathering of the Jews and the creation of their modern nation would lead to a clash between political zionism and Arab nationalism. Few members of the Church fully appreciate the dimensions of this confrontation."
    In what has become a classic address, President Howard W. Hunter observed, "Our Father loves all of his children. He desires all of them to embrace the gospel and come unto him. Only those are favored who obey him and keep his commandments.
    "As members of the Lord's church, we need to lift our vision beyond personal prejudices. We need to discover the supreme truth that indeed our Father is no respecter of persons. Sometimes we unduly offend brothers and sisters of other nations by assigning exclusiveness to one nationality of people over another.
    "Let me cite, as an example of exclusiveness, the present problem in the Middle East—the conflict between the Arabs and the Jews. We do not need to apologize nor mitigate any of the prophecies concerning the Holy Land. We believe them and declare them to be true. But this does not give us justification to dogmatically pronounce that others of our Father's children are not children of promise . . . Both the Jews and the Arabs are children of our Father. They are both children of promise, and as a church we do not take sides. We have love for and an interest in each. The purpose of the gospel of Jesus Christ is to bring about love, unity, and brotherhood of the highest order." See "Orson Hyde's 1841 Mission to the Holy Land," *Ensign*, October 1991.

To Judah from Joseph

On May 2, 1976, President of The Church of Jesus Christ of Latter-day Saints Ezra Taft Benson addressed a large group of Jews, as well as individuals that included members of the Church and nonmember guests. He began his speech with sharing memories of having visited Israel three times where he met with David Ben-Gurion, Levi Eshkol, and Moshe Dayan, early leaders and founders of the state of Israel. Both Ben-Gurion and Eshkol had expressed interest in the story of Orson Hyde and his dedication of Palestine.

David Ben-Gurion had invited Benson to visit with him in his hospital room where he was recovering from an injury from a bomb. Ben-Gurion asked to "know what the attitude of the Mormons was toward the Jews."[27] Perhaps it was as a result of that conversation that Ben-Gurion at a later meeting said, "You know, there are no people in this world who understand the Jews like the Mormons."[28]

While President Benson acknowledged that both the Jews and the Mormons had experienced persecution and suffering, he emphasized that the relationship went deeper than that, a relationship that was built upon a common heritage. He said:

> We need to know more about the Jews, and the Jews ought to know more about the Mormons. When we understand one another, then perhaps you will understand *why* Ben-Gurion said, "There are no people in the world who understand the Jews like the Mormons."[29]

President Benson pointed out the following "kindred doctrines" that are shared by both the Jews and the members of The Church of Jesus Christ of Latter-day Saints: a "mutual belief in Jehovah, a God of revelation." A "common belief in the Messiah who will come," "reciprocal beliefs in prophets," and "a common commitment to the return of the Jews to the land of Jerusalem in fulfillment of the words of the ancient prophets." He added that "there are many other doctrinal and social similarities."[30]

---

27. Ezra Taft Benson, "A Message to Judah from Joseph," *Ensign*, December 1976.
28. Ibid.
29. Ibid.
30. Ibid.

Benson continued:

> From the very inception of this latter-day work, which claims to be a restoration of the covenants given by God to Abraham, Isaac, and Jacob, this church has had a deep interest in the remnant of the house of Israel, the descendants of Judah.[31]

He pointed out that the interest was built on a sense of kinship. He also told the group that he wished to emphasize that

> *All of his* [Jacob's] *posterity* received the family name designation [of Israel] through the twelve sons. Today it has become common practice to identify only one of his twelve sons, Judah, with the family designation "Israelite" because they have maintained their separate identity . . . As you carefully read the forty-ninth chapter of Genesis, you will find that Jacob, or Israel, pronounced blessings on *all* his twelve sons.[32]

Benson then went on to share the blessings given to both Judah and Joseph, as well as the history of the scattering of Israel. He then declared that Joseph's posterity had been preserved and had kept a record now known as the Book of Mormon. He reminded his audience of Ezekiel's prophecy about the stick of Judah and the stick of Joseph becoming one.

"But what of Judah?" President Benson queried. With great compassion, he recounted the history of the suffering of the Jews. He personally had stood in the ruins of a Jewish ghetto in Poland and had been stricken by what he had seen and the stories he had heard. He visited some of the concentration camps, mass graves, and the crematoriums where it is estimated that six million of the sons and daughters of Judah lost their lives. He said:

> I have been impressed to tears as I visited some of these wanderers, those persecuted and driven sons of our Heavenly Father, my brethren of Judah. Yes, the prophecies regarding the dispersion

31. Ezra Taft Benson, "A Message to Judah from Joseph."
32. Ibid.

and suffering of Judah have been fulfilled. But the gathering and reestablishment of the Jews was also clearly predicted.[33]

Benson explained:

> This predicted gathering has three phases: the gathering of Israel to the land of Zion, the American hemisphere; the return of the ten tribes from the north countries; and the reestablishment of the Jews in Palestine which had been long ago predicted by the prophets in these words: "It shall come to pass in that day, that the Lord shall set his hand again *the second time* to recover the remnant of his people . . . And he shall set up an ensign for the nations, and shall assemble the outcasts of Israel, *and gather together the dispersed of Judah from the four corners of the earth*" (Isa. 11:11–12).[34]

It must have been an awe-inspiring moment when President Benson declared:

> To you, our friends of modern Judah, we declare, "We are Joseph, your brothers." We claim kinship with you as descendants from our fathers, Abraham, Isaac, and Jacob. We belong to the same family. We, too, are the house of Israel.[35]

President Benson closed his address with an apostolic blessing:

> As one who, by special assignment, has been given authority in the house of Israel today, I ask the God of Abraham, Isaac and Jacob to bless my brethren of Judah and have mercy on them; that the land to which Judah has returned after a long night of dispersion shall be fruitful, prosperous, and become the envy to her neighbors; that the nation Israel shall be delivered from all her oppressors and enemies; that Judah will "draw water out of the wells of salvation" (Isaiah 12:3) and fulfill all those prophecies that God declared through his prophets Isaiah, Ezekiel and Jeremiah, even that prophecy through Zechariah that "the Lord shall inherit Judah his portion in the holy land, and shall choose Jerusalem again" (Zech. 2:12).[36]

---

33. Ibid.
34. Ibid.
35. Ibid.
36. Ibid.

CHAPTER 25

Healing the Breach

To Look upon the Heart

The relationship between individual members of The Church of Jesus Christ of Latter-day Saints representing the tribe of Joseph and the individual members of the tribe of Judah varies from person to person and is often based upon how much each knows about the other.

Ignorance too often breeds fear and contempt, or even a false sense of superiority, when someone believes he "knows" more than someone else; or worse, when he believes he knows someone's heart when in reality he is entirely in the dark.

We must learn one another's history and look upon the heart as God has instructed. We must look to Joseph and Judah in Egypt and follow their pattern of forgiveness and unity of purpose in behalf of their family as we, too, seek to heal the breach within Israel's family.

Once having been blinded by jealousy, Judah had been the one to sell Joseph, but he also attempted to save his brother from those who wanted to kill him. Judah was also the brother to offer himself as a ransom and a lifelong servant when Joseph discovered the hidden cup in Benjamin's saddlebag. He was willing to sacrifice everything for his family.

Joseph, on the other hand, frankly forgave his brothers and recognized that God had sent him ahead of them in order to save their lives. He held no anger or resentment for their former youthful treatment of him but rather rejoiced in their reunion. He saved their lives with needed food and provided a home for them in Egypt.

The family of Israel is a family of brothers (and sisters), and like all families, there is often misunderstanding and conflict. Yet, both Judah and Joseph recognized the importance of holding their family together, and both accepted leadership roles in accomplishing that goal—roles that included personal sacrifice for the good of others, including the often overlooked brothers whose names are repeated less often.

In order to unite the family of Israel, we must be willing to sacrifice our pride and our judgmental attitudes. We must be willing to embrace the idea that each of the tribes has something essential to offer. We must understand that we are not complete without one another. Judah cannot fill Joseph's role, and Joseph cannot fill Judah's. In addition, it is not the intent that Judah should "become" Joseph, or Joseph, Judah. Each is to maintain his unique perspective and gifts while united under a covenant bond with the God of Israel. This is true for each of the twelve tribes of Israel.

Eventually, as promised, numerous records are yet to come forth from the various tribes, and we must make a place in our heart to receive them. We know that this openness must be extended to all of God's children: we must honor the truth and the light that is in each one.

Elder D. Todd Christofferson urged:

> We cannot permit any racism, tribal prejudice, or other divisions to exist in the latter-day Church of Christ. The Lord commands us, "Be one; and if ye are not one ye are not mine."[1] We should be diligent in rooting prejudice and discrimination out of the Church, out of our homes, and, most of all, out of our hearts.[2]

1. Doctrine and Covenants 38:27.
2. D. Todd Christofferson, "The Doctrine of Belonging," *Ensign*, November 2022.

The Messiah, Jesus Christ, Is the Healer of the Breach and the Hope of Israel

Even as King David united the tribes of Israel, so the Jewish Son of David, who is Jesus Christ, will be the binding power that will unite the tribes again. Then Joseph (or Ephraim) and Judah, both given blessings of leadership, will come to see how their leadership roles are fulfilled as they gather and prepare a people to live under the reign of Jesus Christ. Jesus, who is Jehovah, is the Holy One of Israel, the Great Healer of the Breach,[3] and the Hope *of* Israel.

From Judah came the Messiah, as well as a deep love and reverence for the ancient covenants and the temple. From Judah came "*The Book*"—the Old Testament (or Torah), which contains the covenants and the prophecies concerning the family of Israel. The promises made to Israel are eternal, and they are recorded and have their origin in the Old Testament record. They are vital to our understanding of what it means to be a covenant people.

We might say that from Judah also came the New Testament, the record and witness of the Son of David, the Messiah, Jesus Christ.

From Ephraim, or Joseph, comes the Book of Mormon, the Prophet Joseph Smith, and the Restoration of ancient covenants. One of the purposes of the Book of Mormon is to remind Israel of her covenants and to testify that the Lord has not forgotten them. The title page of the Book of Mormon states:

> Written to the Lamanites, who are a remnant of the house of Israel; and also to Jew and Gentile—Written by way of commandment, and also by the spirit of prophecy and revelation—Written and sealed up and hid up unto the Lord, that they might not be destroyed—To come forth by the gift and power of God unto the interpretation thereof—Sealed by the hand of Moroni, and hid up unto the Lord, to come forth in due time by way of the Gentile—The interpretation thereof by the gift of God . . .
>
> . . . Which is to show unto the remnant of the house of Israel what great things the Lord hath done for their fathers; and that they may

3. See Isaiah 58:12.

> know the covenants of the Lord, that they are not cast off forever—and also to the convincing of the Jew and Gentile that JESUS is the CHRIST, the ETERNAL GOD, manifesting himself unto all nations.

Each of these sacred records and the tribes who authored them are essential to the wellbeing of God's covenant family of Israel. As Ezekiel prophesied when it came to seeing new life for Israel, these records must become one in our hand,[4] both equally cherished for the continuous golden thread of truth to which they testify.

All Are Invited

Let us never forget that it is God's eternal plan that every one of His children be invited to become a member of His covenant family of Israel. Regardless of race or gender, all are alike unto God, and all are invited.

> He doeth nothing save it be plain unto the children of men; and he inviteth them all to come unto him and partake of his goodness; and he denieth none that come unto him, black and white, bond and free, male and female; and he remembereth the heathen; and all are alike unto God, both Jew and Gentile.[5]

As recorded in the New Testament, Peter, a Jew, was amazed when the Lord directed him to take the gospel covenant and its blessings to Cornelius, a Roman centurion. Although as a Jew Peter had been taught that he was not even to share a meal with a Gentile, he allowed the Spirit to soften his heart, taught and baptized Cornelius, and then rejoiced that God had opened the doors for the Gentiles to come into the covenant fold.[6]

Today, as Gentiles, we must also have open hearts to those who are coming into the fold of Christ and remember that none are forbidden. There is much to gain as new members come to the fold and bring their culture and traditions with them. For example, many Jewish

4. See Ezekiel 37.
5. 2 Nephi 26:33.
6. See Acts 10.

members of the Church share that remembering and celebrating the ancient holy days, and reciting the Torah in Hebrew helps them have a deeper understanding and testimony of the restored gospel today. Their knowledge could be helpful to us as we remember the prophecies that we will all celebrate the ancient Israelite holy days of Passover and Tabernacles during the Millennium.[7]

In *The Burning Book*, Jason Olson shares his journey of faith as a Jew who converts to Christianity and The Church of Jesus Christ of Latter-day Saints. Jason brings his "Jewishness" with him to enrich his understanding of what many members of the Church miss if the Church is all they've known. Jason's love for and understanding of Old Testament prophets, covenant making, and the temple deeply expand his view of modern prophecy and the restored temple covenants of today.[8] There is much that members of the Church can learn from converts like Jason with his rich heritage of faith based upon being a member of covenant Israel.

Surely there will be more to be restored and remembered as we obtain the records and traditions of the other tribes and members of Israel. President Russell M. Nelson reminded us, "We're witnesses to a process of restoration. If you think the Church has been fully restored, you're just seeing the beginning. There is much more to come."[9]

Children of the Covenant

We must understand what it is to be children of the covenant. President Nelson explained, "When we realize that we are children of the covenant, we know who we are and what God expects of us. His law is written in our hearts. He is our God and we are His people."[10]

What *does* God expect of us as children of the covenant?

God referred to Abraham as his "friend" and said of him:

---

7. See Lynda Cherry's *The Feasts and Festivals of the Messiah*; Zechariah 14:16.
8. Jason Olson and James Goldberg, *The Burning Book.*
9. Tad Walch, "What we learned from President Russell M. Nelson's South American ministry," thechurchnews.com, November 8, 2018.
10. Russell M. Nelson, "Covenants," *Ensign*, November 2011.

> For I know him [Abraham], that he will command his children and his household after him, and they shall keep the way of the Lord, to do justice and judgment; that the Lord may bring upon Abraham that which he hath spoken of him.[11]

Note the important qualifications the Lord attributed to Abraham's worthiness to become the "Father of the Covenant." The Lord *knew* that Abraham would not only honor and keep the covenant promises that he had made, but he would also most certainly teach his children to do likewise.

In fact, Abraham *did* confer his own characteristics of steady faith and commitment upon his birthright son, Isaac, who willingly complied with the sacrifice at Mount Moriah and did not resist when his father laid him upon the altar.[12] Furthermore, Isaac had his own personal encounter with the Lord where he renewed the covenant that his father Abraham had made.[13]

Jacob, Isaac's birthright son, inherited the birthright promises of the priesthood through which the "Abrahamic" promises were to be fulfilled.[14] His elder twin brother, Esau, had disregarded the covenant promises, because they meant little to him.[15] But Jacob earned his rights not only as a direct descendant of Abraham and Isaac, but also by his diligence and faithfulness in seeking after righteousness. He saw "the gate of heaven," encountered the Lord, and following the pattern set for him, had his own personal experience of committing himself through covenant to God and therefore likewise received the covenant promises.[16]

Jacob, like Abraham, adhered to the covenants that he had made with the Lord and taught his children to do the same. Some years after his initial encounter with the Lord at "the gate of heaven," Jacob met an angel who blessed him and changed his name to Israel.[17] From

---

11. Genesis 18:19.
12. See Genesis 22:7–10.
13. See Genesis 26:1–6, 24–25.
14. See Abraham 2.
15. See Genesis 26:34–35.
16. See Genesis 28:11–17.
17. See Genesis 32:24–28.

that point on, "Israel" became the name of God's covenant family. According to the footnote for Genesis 32:28, the name "Israel" means "He perseveres (with) God; it may also mean, Let God prevail."

It would appear, then, that children of the covenant seek to know God for themselves and bind themselves to Him through covenant promises and ordinances. They also teach their children about the covenants that have come down through the ages and encourage them to have their own personal relationship with the Lord. They love God with all of their heart, soul, and mind, and they love their neighbors to a degree that they seek to bless and lift them and to invite them to participate in the blessings of the covenant as well.[18]

What Is the Abrahamic Covenant?

What was the covenant given to Abraham, and how does that covenant pertain to us today? It is well for us to review the promises and ponder the question, "Am I, as did Abraham, Isaac, and Jacob, fulfilling the duty of teaching my children to walk in the covenant and to seek their own experience in renewing it personally with the Lord?" To Abraham, the Lord said:

> My name is Jehovah, and I know the end from the beginning; therefore my hand shall be over thee. And I will make of thee a great nation, and I will bless thee above measure, and make thy name great among all nations, and thou shalt be a blessing unto thy seed after thee, that in their hands they shall bear this ministry and Priesthood unto all nations;
>
> And I will bless them through thy name; for as many as receive this Gospel shall be called after thy name, and shall be accounted thy seed, and shall rise up and bless thee, as their father; And I will bless them that bless thee, and curse them that curse thee; and in thee (that is, in thy Priesthood) and in thy seed (that is, thy Priesthood), for I give unto thee a promise that this right shall continue in thee, and in thy seed after thee (that is to say, the literal seed, or the seed of the body) shall all the families of the earth be blessed, even with

18. Matthew 22:37–39.

the blessings of the Gospel, which are the blessings of salvation, even of life eternal.[19]

Russell M. Nelson explained:

> The covenant that the Lord first made to Abraham and reaffirmed to Isaac and Jacob is of transcendent significance. It contained several promises:
>
> - Abraham's posterity would be numerous, entitled to eternal increase and to bear the priesthood.
> - He would become a father of many nations.
> - Christ and kings would come through Abraham's lineage.
> - Certain lands would be inherited.
> - All nations of the earth would be blessed by his seed.
> - That covenant would be everlasting—even through "a thousand generations."[20]

Even though the children of Israel stray and experience difficult consequences as a result, the Lord does not depart from His promises. As Nephi testified, the Lord will remember His covenants forever[21] because of the faithfulness of Abraham and others who have gone before us. These promises are sure. However, we are each invited to have a personal experience and witness and to enter into a firsthand covenant with the Lord.

The Seed of Abraham to Bless the Families of the Earth

One of the promises to Abraham that pertains to our question as to how we can heal the breach of splintered Israel is that the Lord promised that through Abraham's seed (and priesthood), all the families of the earth would be blessed, "even with the blessings of the

---

19. Abraham 2:8–11.
20. Russell M. Nelson, "Children of the Covenant," *Ensign*, May 1995.
21. 2 Nephi 29:14.

Gospel, which are the blessings of salvation, even of life eternal."[22] As we develop our own relationship with God, make and keep our covenants, and have a heart filled with the desire to bless others, we can have the love of God course through us with its own healing light and power.

Corrie Ten Boom shared a personal story that illustrates how this principle works. Corrie and her sister, Betsie, hid Jews in Holland during World War II. They were discovered, arrested, and sent to Ravensbruck, a concentration camp where their father and Betsie died.

After the war, Corrie was speaking to Germans about Jesus Christ and the power of His love and forgiveness when a man she recognized as a former Nazi soldier who had been a guard at Ravensbruck approached her. He did not recognize her, but she remembered him as the first of their jailers in the processing rooms, which included the dreaded showers.

He held out his hand to her and told her that he had become a Christian since the war. He asked her if she could forgive him for what he had done as a Nazi. For a few moments, Corrie was frozen as she remembered Betsie's humiliation and suffering. She knew that Jesus had said that all must forgive, but she wondered how she could do it with this man who represented the worst that they had endured. Corrie began to pray silently, "Jesus, help me! I can lift my hand. I can do that much. You supply the feeling."

Corrie recorded:

> As I took his hand, the most incredible thing happened. From my shoulder along my arm and through my hand a current seemed to pass from me to him, while into my heart sprang a love for this stranger that almost overwhelmed me. And so I discovered that it is not on our forgiveness any more than on our goodness that the world's healing hinges, but on His. When He tells us to love our enemies, He gives, along with the command, the love itself.[23]

---

22. Abraham 2:8–11.
23. Corrie Ten Boom, *The Hiding Place*, 215.

If we ask, God will provide the love and the forgiveness and will also bring the healing. We just need to be willing.

CHAPTER 26

Judah and Joseph Reunited: The Hope for Israel

And he shall set up an ensign for the nations,
and shall assemble the outcasts of Israel,
and gather together the dispersed of Judah
from the four corners of the earth.
The envy also of Ephraim shall depart,
and the adversaries of Judah shall be cut off:
Ephraim shall not envy Judah,
and Judah shall not vex Ephraim.[1]

Isaiah prophesies of the day when Judah and Ephraim will join together again as brothers, their envy and jealousy ended. The two brothers and their successive tribal families were given blessings of leadership in their patriarchal blessings received from their father, Jacob, or Israel.[2]

They, and their posterity, may have wondered how both brothers could be leaders at the same time. Their positions in the fore-guard and rear-guard of the camp of Israel acknowledged their unique roles

1. Isaiah 11:12–13; 2 Nephi 21:12–13.
2. See Genesis 49–50.

as principals in Israel and were also symbolic of the *timing* of their roles.

Judah and Ephraim had equal responsibilities, though different, in the front and rear of Israel's camp. As they made their way into the promised land, Judah (in Joshua) and Ephraim (in Caleb) led all of the other tribes. Judah was given the first land allotment, followed next by Joseph, or Ephraim and Manasseh. Judah was given the holy city of Jerusalem, and Ephraim had Bethel and Shiloh, both sacred sites.

Judaic King David united all of Israel under God and under covenant, with the temple at the center of daily life, but Ephraimite Jeroboam divided Israel and undermined the temple, which led to the destruction and scattering of the ten tribes. However, in their scattering, Ephraim and Manasseh (Joseph) have played essential roles in God's covenant plan.

Judah has been under bondage far too long, and Jehovah has promised their release and renewal. He has called upon Ephraim under the direction of Joseph Smith and The Church of Jesus Christ of Latter-day Saints to awaken the world to the plight of the Jews (and the other lost tribes). Under Joseph Smith's direction, Jerusalem and the Holy Land have been dedicated for the return of the Jews, and they are returning.

The bulk of the responsibility for gathering Israel lies on the shoulders of Ephraim, who has the birthright priesthood responsibility, even like Joseph of old, to minister to *all* the tribes of Israel. The twelve oxen under the brazen sea in ancient and modern temples testify of this important duty. As many foresaw, Ephraim's (Joseph's) greatest leadership was to occur in the latter days in the role of the Gentiles who would bring the restored covenant and gospel blessings back to Judah and all of Israel, and, in fact, to the entire family of Abraham and beyond.[3]

But this does not mean that Ephraim *supplants* Judah—far from it. The two brothers must combine their knowledge and their love in bringing the truths of Jehovah to all the world.

---

3. See Isaiah 49:22–23.

Judah is also a significant leader in the gathering as they add their knowledge to the Restoration taking place and look to prepare themselves and Jerusalem for the coming Messiah. Regardless of the world's judgment, the Lord has declared that the Jews are "His" people, and He will defend them and live in their midst during the Millennium.

The arrangement of the camp of Israel, with Judah and Ephraim at the front and rear, may foreshadow the Millennium when the Messiah from the tribe of Judah—Jesus Christ—will reign from Jerusalem and Ephraim (or Joseph) has the responsibility to build the New Jerusalem, or Zion.[4]

Even as Judah and Joseph do not supplant one another, so they do not supplant the important individuality of any of the other tribes of Israel or of those who choose not to become a part of the covenant Israelite family at all. This is not a racial treatise, but rather an explanation of the ongoing responsibilities of the two leaders of the family of Israel. Individuality and agency are cherished aspects of God's plan of happiness.

To summarize: *Why are Joseph and Judah appointed roles of leadership at all? And why do those blessings, pronounced thousands of years ago, still have application?*

God loves His children. He is our Father. He yearns for us to return to His presence and become like Him. To accomplish those purposes, He instituted the Plan of Salvation, with the Atonement of the Messiah, Jesus Christ, as its activating agent. Jesus *did* perform the Atonement for all mankind so that if they will, they can overcome sin and death and fulfill the measure of their creation.

Even as Jesus was foreordained in the premortal world to fulfill His mission as Savior and Redeemer, so each of us has been foreordained to fulfill certain missions as well. Joseph Smith taught, "Every man [and woman] who has a calling to minister to the inhabitants of the world was ordained to that very purpose in the grand council of heaven before this world was."[5]

Judah and Joseph were foreordained for their missions as individuals. This is particularly marked in Joseph's declaration to his brothers

4. See Isaiah 2:3

5. Joseph Smith, *History of the Church*, 6:364.

that God had sent him ahead of them in order to preserve their lives.[6] Having this clarity about his role enabled Joseph to find strength and courage in the most difficult of circumstances. Knowing our own role can provide the same strength and clarity for each of us.

The promises made to Judah and Joseph as individuals continue on through their tribal families. Each of the tribes received blessings that are still in effect that include duties for us as their descendants. As we seek for understanding of those responsibilities, God will give us the courage and vision to partner with Him in His work. That work is to gather and unite His family under the covenant of Christ and to prepare them for the coming of the Messiah.

Remember Rabbi Israel's understanding of a reading of the *Zohar* that "a reunion between the lost ten tribes of Israel and the children of Judah was necessary before the Messiah would come and redeem His people."[7] Rabbi Israel and his fellows, representing Judah, recognized that important truth, as did Joseph Smith (representing Joseph and Ephraim) in his day. Both felt this call and testimony around the same year: 1830.

Even as Judah could not bear the thought of leaving Benjamin behind in Egypt when Joseph tested his loyalty, we cannot bear the thought now of leaving anyone out. We must be a united family of covenant faith, centered on our love of God—Jehovah, or Jesus Christ the Messiah.

This unity of purpose, faith, and love is essential to our ultimate goal of receiving the Messiah. Rabbi Immanuel Schochet taught that Messiah ben Joseph must precede Messiah ben Judah and prepare the way for the final reign of Messiah ben Judah.[8] That time is now. This truth is reason to rejoice and reason to "wake up," prepare, and help share the good news. We are preparing hearts (and our homes) to receive the Messiah!

Jesus Christ, the Messiah, is the Hope *of* Israel. Judah and Joseph reunited is the hope *for* Israel in gathering and restoring all of the

---

6. Genesis 45:5.
7. "Vilna Gaon's Students Letter to the Lost Tribes," sefaria.org.; "Letter to the Ten Lost Tribes of Israel," safaria.org.
8. Immanuel Schochet, "Messiah ben Yossef."

truths ancient and modern. This gathering of truth will have a natural effect of calling God's people back to Him.

> Yea, let the cry go forth among all people: Awake and arise and go forth to meet the Bridegroom; behold and lo, the Bridegroom cometh; go ye out to meet him. Prepare yourselves for the great day of the Lord . . . And the Lord, even the Savior, shall stand in the midst of his people, and shall reign over all flesh.
>
> And they who are in the north countries shall come in remembrance before the Lord; and their prophets shall hear his voice, and shall no longer stay themselves; and they shall smite the rocks, and the ice shall flow down at their presence. And an highway shall be cast up in the midst of the great deep. Their enemies shall become a prey unto them, And in the barren deserts there shall come forth pools of living water; and the parched ground shall no longer be a thirsty land.
>
> And they shall bring forth their rich treasures unto the children of Ephraim, my servants, and the boundaries of the everlasting hills shall tremble at their presence. And there shall they fall down and be crowned with glory, even in Zion, by the hands of the servants of the Lord, even the children of Ephraim. And they shall be filled with songs of everlasting joy.
>
> Behold, this is the blessing of the everlasting God upon the tribes of Israel, and the richer blessing upon the head of Ephraim and his fellows.
>
> And they also of the tribe of Judah, after their pain, shall be sanctified in holiness before the Lord, to dwell in his presence day and night, forever and ever.
>
> And now, verily saith the Lord, that these things might be known among you, O inhabitants of the earth, I have sent forth mine angel flying through the midst of heaven, having the everlasting gospel, who hath appeared unto some and hath committed it unto man, who shall appear unto many that dwell on the earth. And this gospel shall be preached unto every nation, and kindred, and tongue, and people.[9]

9. Doctrine and Covenants 133:10, 25–37.

Bibliography

Allen, J. H. *Judah's Sceptre and Joseph's Birthright, an Analysis of the Prophecies of the Scriptures in Regard to the Royal Family of Judah and the Many Nations of Israel, the Lost Ten Tribes*. Merrimack, MA: Destiny, 1917.

Altein, Yehuda. "The High Priest's Breastplate," chabad.org.

Anderson, Bernhard W. *Understanding the Old Testament*. Upper Saddle River, NJ: Pearson, 1986.

Ballard, M. Russell. "The Miracle of the Bible." *Ensign*, May 2007. Salt Lake City: The Church of Jesus Christ of Latter-day Saints, churchofjesuschrist.org.

Barker, Margaret. "What Did King Josiah Reform?," scholarsarchive.byu.edu, 2003.

Barrett, LaMar C., and Blair G. VanDyke "In the Footsteps of Orson Hyde: Subsequent Dedications of the Holy Land," BYU Studies, 47:1, 57, byustudies.byu.edu.

Benson, Ezra T. "A Message to Judah from Joseph." *Ensign*, December 1976. Salt Lake City: The Church of Jesus Christ of Latter-day Saints, churchofjesuschrist.org.

bible.usccb.org. United States Conference of Catholic Bishops.

bible.ucg.org (see also updated site ucg.org). United Church of God. "The Stunning Death of Judah's Most Righteous King."

Birnbaum, Eli. *Beyond Time, Beyond Place*, jewishhistory.org.il.

Bradshaw, Jeffrey M. "What Was the Religious Role of Music in the Life and Times of David?," interpreterfoundation.org., 2018.

Bradshaw, Jeffrey M. "How Should We Understand the Symbolism in Jacob's Blessing of Judah and Joseph?" *Meridian Magazine*, latterdaysaintmag.com, 2018.

Bradshaw, Robert I. "Deuteronomy," biblicalstudies.org.uk.

Bradshaw, Robert I. "The Babylonian Exile of Israel," biblical studies.org.uk.

British Library, "Expulsion of Jews from England, 1290," bl.uk.

Butterick, George. *The Interpreter's Dictionary of the Bible.* Nashville: Abingdon, 1966.

Brown, Matthew B. *The Gate of Heaven.* American Fork, UT: Covenant, 2014.

Brown, S. Kent, and Richard Neitzel Holzapfel. *Between the Testaments: From Malachi to Matthew.* Salt Lake City: Deseret Book, 2002.

Carew, Mairead. *Tara and the Ark of the Covenant.* Dublin: Royal Irish Academy, 2003.

Cherry, Lynda. *The Redemption of the Bride: God's Redeeming Love for His Covenant People.* Springville, UT: Cedar Fort, 2022.

Cherry, Lynda. *The Feasts and Festivals of the Messiah.* Springville, UT: Cedar Fort, 2022.

Church News, thechurchnews.com. Salt Lake City: The Church of Jesus Christ of Latter-day Saints and the *Deseret News.*

Christofferson, D. Todd. "The Doctrine of Belonging." *Ensign*, November 2022. Salt Lake City: The Church of Jesus Christ of Latter-day Saints, churchofjesus-christ.org.

Craigie, Peter C. *The Book of Deuteronomy.* Grand Rapids: MI: Eerdmans, 1976.

Dialogue, dialoguejournal.com.

Draper, Richard D. "The Prophets of the Exile; Saviors of a People." *Sperry Symposium Classics: The Old Testament.* Salt Lake City: Deseret Book and Brigham Young University, 2005, rsc.byu.edu.

Edersheim, Alfred. *Bible History, Old Testament.* Peabody, MA: Hendrickson Academic, 1994.

Encyclopedia Judaica. 16th ed., 16 vols. Jerusalem, Israel: Keter, 1971.

Ensign. Salt Lake City: The Church of Jesus Christ of Latter-day Saints.

Epperson, Steven. "Jews in the Columns of Joseph's *Times and Seasons.*" *Dialogue*, Volume 22, No. 4, dialoguejournal.com.

Facing History and Ourselves, facinghistory.org.

FAIR (Faithful Answers, Informed Responses), fairlatterdaysaints.org.

Faithful Answers, Informed Responses. "The Book of Mormon and the Stick of Ephraim," fairlatterdaysaints.org.

Flannery, Edward H. *The Anguish of the Jews.* Mahwah, NJ: Paulist, 2004.

Galbraith, David. "Orson Hyde's 1841 Mission to the Holy Land," *Ensign*, October 1991. Salt Lake City: The Church of Jesus Christ of Latter-day Saints, churchofjesuschrist.org.

Ginzberg, Louis. *The Legend of the Jews.* Philadelphia, PA: Jewish Publication Society, 2003.

Glover, Frederick Robert Augustus. *England, the Remnant of Judah and the Israel of Ephraim: The Two Families Under One Head; a Hebrew Episode in British History.* Whitefish, MT: Kessinger, 2010.

Goldberg, James, and Jason Olson. "The Burning Book." Newburgh, IN: Common Consent, 2022.

Hamblin, William. "Vindicating Josiah." *Interpreter: A Journal of Latter-day Saint Faith and Scholarship,* 4 (2013), interpreterfoundation.org.

Hay, Malcolm. *Europe and the Jews.* Chicago, IL: Academy Chicago, 2005.

History, history.com. "Spain Announces It Will Expel All Jews."

Holzapfel, Richard Neitzel, and S. Kent Brown. *Between the Testaments: From Malachi to Matthew.* Salt Lake City: Deseret Book, 2002.

Jewish History, jewishhistory.org.

Jews for Judaism, jewsforjudaism.org. "The Stick of Judah and the Stick of Joseph."

Josephus, Flavius. *Antiquities of the Jews.* Foxboro, MA: Foxboro Press, 2006.

Josephus, Flavius. *Wars of the Jews.* Digireads.com, 2020.

Journal of Discourses. 26 vols. London: Latter-day Saints' Book Depot, 1854–86.

Ludlow, Daniel. "Of the House of Israel." *Ensign*, January 1991. Salt Lake City: The Church of Jesus Christ of Latter-day Saints, churchofjesuschrist.org.

Ludlow, Daniel. "What laws governed the inheritance of birthright in the Old Testament?" *Ensign*, September 1980. Salt Lake City: The Church of Jesus Christ of Latter-day Saints, churchofjesuschrist.org.

Maimonides (Moses ben Maimon [1138–1204]). *Selected Works of Moses Maimonides: Sha'arei Zedeq le-Zera Yizhaq* (*Gates of Righteousness*). Publishers: Jewish Publication Society, Bloch Publishing, American Academy for Jewish Research, and others, 1903–1938.

Madsen, Ann N., and N. Barnard. "Judah Through the Centuries." *Ensign*, January 1982. Salt Lake City: The Church of Jesus Christ of Latter-day Saints, churchofjesuschrist.org.

Meridian Magazine, latterdaysaintmag.com.

Meservy, Keith. "Ezekiel's Sticks and the Gathering of Israel." *Ensign,* February 1987. Salt Lake City: The Church of Jesus Christ of Latter-day Saints, churchofjesuschrist.org.

Mindei, Nissan. "Gedaliah." Kehot Publication Society, chabad.org.

Morgenstern, Arie. *Hastening Redemption: Messianism and the Resettlement of the Land of Israel.* Oxford, England: Oxford University, 2006.

Nelson, Russell M. "The Gathering of Scattered Israel." *Ensign*, November 2006. Salt Lake City: The Church of Jesus Christ of Latter-day Saints, churchofjesus-christ.org.

Nelson, Russell M. "Children of the Covenant." *Ensign*, May 1995. Salt Lake City: The Church of Jesus Christ of Latter-day Saints, churchofjesuschrist.org.

Nelson, Russell M. "Covenants." *Ensign*, November 2011. Salt Lake City: The Church of Jesus Christ of Latter-day Saints, churchofjesuschrist.org.

Old Testament Student Manual. Salt Lake City: The Church of Jesus Christ of Latter-day Saints, churchofjesuschrist.org.

Olson, Jason, and James Goldberg. "The Burning Book." Newburgh, IN: Common Consent, 2022.

Peterson, Daniel C. "Nephi and His Asherah." *Journal of Book of Mormon Studies*, Volume 9, Number 2, July 31, 2000.

Ringwood, Michael T. "For God So Loved Us." *Ensign*, May 2022. Salt Lake City: The Church of Jesus Christ of Latter-day Saints, churchofjesuschrist.org.

Schochet, Immanuel. "Mashiach ben Yossef, " chabad.org.

Schochet, Immanuel. "The Prophet Elijah: Harbinger of the Redemption," https://www.chabad.org/library/article_cdo/aid/101746/jewish/The-Prophet-Elijah-Harbinger-of-the-Redemption.htm.

Seely, David R. and JoAnn H. Seely. "Lehi and Jeremiah: Prophets, Priests, and Patriarchs." *Journal of Book of Mormon Studies,* 8/2, 1999, scholarsarchive.byu.edu.

Sefaria, sefaria.org.

Showers, Renald. "Babylon and Medo-Persia." The Friends of Israel Gospel Ministry, August/September 1994, israelmyglory.org.

Sloyan, Gerard S. "Christian Persecution of Jews over the Centuries." United States Holocaust Memorial Museum, ushmm.org.

Smith, Joseph. *History of the Church of Jesus Christ of Latter-day Saints.* Salt Lake City: Deseret Book, 1978.

Smith, Joseph Fielding. *The Restoration of All Things.* Salt Lake City: Deseret News Publishing, 1944.

Smith, Joseph Fielding. *Answers to Gospel Questions.* Compiled by Joseph Fielding Smith. 5 vols. Salt Lake City: Deseret Book, 1957–66.

Smith, Joseph Fielding. *Doctrines of Salvation.* Compiled by Bruce R. McConkie. 3 vols. Salt Lake City: Bookcraft, 1954–56.

Sorenson, John L. "The 'Mulekites.'" *BYU Studies Quarterly,* Volume 30, Issue 3, Article 8, scholarsarchive.byu.edu.

Strong, James. *New Strong's Concordance of the Bible.* Nashville: Thomas Nelson, 2010.

Talmage, James E. *House of the Lord: A Study of Holy Sanctuaries Ancient and Modern.* Salt Lake City: Bookcraft, 1971.

Ten Boom, Corrie. *The Hiding Place.* Uhrichsville, OH: Barbour, 1971.

Times and Seasons, March 15, 1842, edition.

United Church of God, ucg.org (see also bible.ucg.org). "The Stunning Death of Judah's Most Righteous King."

United States Holocaust Memorial Museum, ushmm.org.

VanDyke, Blair G. and LaMar C. Barrett. "In the Footsteps of Orson Hyde: Subsequent Dedications of the Holy Land." *BYU Studies,* 47:1, byustudies.byu.edu.

Walch, Tad. "What we learned from President Russell M. Nelson's South American ministry," thechurchnews.com, November 8, 2018.

West Coast Chabad Lubavitch, chabad.com.

Wild, Joseph. *The Lost Ten Tribes and 1882.* The Project Gutenberg eBook, released November 6, 2008, transcribed from the 1880 Robert Banks edition, gutenberg.org., 2008.

Winkle, Ross E. "Jeremiah's Seventy Years for Babylon: A Re-Assessment, Part I: The Scriptural Data." Andrews University Seminary Studies, Summer 1987, Vol. 25, No. 2. Andrews University, digitalcommons.andrews.edu, 1987.

Winkler, Albert. "The Medieval Holocaust: The Approach of the Plague and the Destruction of Jews in Germany, 1348–49." BYU Scholars Archive, Brigham Young University, scholarsarchive.byu.edu, 2005.

Notes

Notes

Notes

Notes

Notes

About the Author

Lynda Cherry is the author of *The Redemption of the Bride: God's Redeeming Love for His Covenant People* and *The Feasts and Festivals of the Messiah,* as well as *A Passover Seder Script for Christian Families.* She is the host of the *Come Follow Me Made Easier* podcast presented by Cedar Fort Publishing and Media.

As a convert and active member of The Church of Jesus Christ of Latter-day Saints for more than forty years, Lynda brings with her a remarkable insight and a rich heritage. With her background of evangelistic Christianity, combined with her love of the Jewish people and her desire to gather all into the family of covenant Israel, she possesses a unique perspective that greatly enhances her work. She seeks to build bridges of connection, unity, and understanding between the different faith groups and demonstrate the fulfillment of covenant promises through the Restoration.

Lynda has taught BYU Continuing Education, institute, seminary, and adult education classes, as well as Gospel Doctrine for more than thirty years. She has been a guest lecturer at BYU Education Week and B'Nai Shalom and has presented many firesides. She has led tour groups to the Holy Lands of Egypt, Jordan, and Israel. She has served as president of the Relief Society, Young Women, and Primary organizations of The Church of Jesus Christ of Latter-day Saints.

Scan to visit

lyndacherrybooksandtours.com

AUTHORS WANTED

You've dreamed of accomplishing your publishing goal for ages—holding *that* book in your hands. We want to partner with you in bringing this dream to light.

Whether you're an aspiring author looking to publish your first book or a seasoned author who's been published before, we want to hear from you. Please submit your manuscript to:

CEDARFORT.SUBMITTABLE.COM/SUBMIT

CEDAR FORT
Publishing & Media

CEDAR FORT IS CURRENTLY PUBLISHING BOOKS IN THE FOLLOWING GENRES:

- LDS Nonfiction
- General Nonfiction
- Biographies
- Children's
- Comic & Activity books
- Self-Help
- Children's books with customizable characters